SUFFERING
IS
OPTIONAL

THREE KEYS TO FREEDOM AND JOY

CHERI HUBER

Also by Cheri Huber

From Keep It Simple Books
Transform Your Life: A Year of Awareness Practice (Fall 2007)
The Key and the Name of the Key Is Willingness
That Which You Are Seeking Is Causing You to Seek
How You Do Anything Is How You Do Everything: A Workbook
There Is Nothing Wrong With You: Going Beyond Self-Hate
There Is Nothing Wrong With You for Teens
The Depression Book: Depression as an Opportunity for Spiritual Growth
The Fear Book: Facing Fear Once and for All
Nothing Happens Next: Responses to Questions about Meditation
Be the Person You Want to Find: Relationship and Self-Discovery
Suffering Is Optional: Three Keys to Freedom and Joy
When You're Falling, Dive: Acceptance, Possibility and Freedom
Time-Out for Parents: A Guide to Compassionate Parenting, Rev. Ed.
Trying to Be Human: Zen Talks (Sara Jenkins, editor)
Good Life: A Zen Precepts Retreat with Cheri Huber (Sara Jenkins, editor)
Buddha Facing the Wall (Sara Jenkins, editor)
Sweet Zen: Dharma Talks with Cheri Huber (Sara Jenkins, editor)
The Zen Monastery Cookbook: Stories and Recipes from a Zen Kitchen

From Hay House
How to Get from Where You Are to Where You Want to Be

From Shambhala Publications
Making a Change for Good: A Guide to Compassionate Self-Discipline

DVDs from Openings
(www.yogaopenings.com)
There Are No Secrets: Zen Meditation with Cheri Huber
Yoga for Meditators *with Christa Rypins*
Yoga for A Better Back *with Christa Rypins and Dr. John Sousa*
Yummy Yoga: Stress Relief for Hips, Back, and Neck *with Christa Rypins*

Published by Keep It Simple Books
Printed in the United States of America

ISBN 0-9636255-8-6

Cover design by Mary Denkinger
Cover art by Alex Mill

First Printing, 2000.
Second Printing, 2002
Third Printing 2005
Fourth Printing 2007

Zen Flesh, Zen Bones is published by Anchor Books.
Traveling Mercies is published by Pantheon Books.

This book is offered in gratitude
to all the great teachers
who have transmitted the Dharma
to this holy day.

Thank you to
all who participated in the email class
on which this book is based.

Thank you to
those who have been willing to prove
to themselves that it is possible
to move beyond suffering in this lifetime.

Thank you most especially to
June Shiver
without whose talent, skill,
understanding, and tenacity
our email classes and this book
would not exist.

Preface

This book is the culmination of a twelve-week online class offered in the spring of 2000. There were over 550 participants. Two assignments were emailed each week. Class members did the exercises and then emailed me letting me know what they were noticing. Some assignments elicited many more responses than others. Daily I chose several of the most representative responses (my staff removed the names so the emails were anonymous), replied to them, and sent them to the entire class.

Many hundreds of pages of honest, touching, and exciting work resulted. Paring those hundreds of pages to manageable size required making hard choices. I could probably take much that did not make it into this book and release it as <u>Suffering</u> <u>Is</u> <u>Optional</u>, <u>Vol.</u> <u>2</u>.

The participants in this class honored me greatly by signing up and doing the work. It takes courage to look deeply into oneself, and being asked to help guide the journey always moves me.

C. H.

October 2000

Introduction

What do we mean, "suffering is optional"?

The Buddha taught that suffering exists because old age, sickness, and death are inescapable. Another way of describing suffering is that we want what we don't get, aren't satisfied with what we do get, are separated from those or that which we love, and are forced to endure those and that which we do not love.

As I see it, the whole thing comes down to not getting what we want.

When we don't get what we want, we are miserable. "So what do I do?" we want to know. First, we pay attention to the voice that asks that question. We pay attention to what it is that we want. We pay attention to the experience of feeling miserable when we don't get what we want. We notice and question our beliefs, including the assumption that our problems will all be solved by <u>doing</u>. In that process of noticing and questioning, our attitude changes: We no longer take life so personally. In short, we shift our focus from clinging to the content of our suffering to observing the process.

Already, in that shift, we have ceased to suffer.

Soon enough, however, the suffering will be back. The Buddha's great realization was that suffering arises from a deeply held but mistaken notion that each of us is a fixed, distinct self that is separate from everything else. We call that sense of a separate self "egocentricity" or just "ego." The question, "What do I DO?" is the cry of egocentricity. In fact, there is nothing to do because there is no separate self. The whole idea of "us against life" is an illusion.

Where does that illusion come from? It is instilled in us from birth, through what we are told about the world, what we are taught about how we should be, what we observe in those around us. That is what we call "conditioning," both the process of coming to believe those things and the internalized set of beliefs.

We are conditioned to believe in the illusion that to be acceptable, we must turn away from our own inclinations and follow socially prescribed rules. Our conditioning is so pervasive that it can be difficult to see. But that is what we do in this practice of awareness: We observe our egocentric conditioning, as the only way to live free from its constraints.

Here's how it works:
We suffer when we resist life. We suffer when we believe life should be different. We suffer when we think there is something wrong with life that needs to be changed or fixed.

Being in a position to judge in that way requires separation from what is being judged, and only egocentric conditioning believes itself to be separate from life. As we see through the illusion of separation, we realize there is no separate self, no alternative reality in which life is different, no other choice, and our suffering falls away.

Only egocentricity suffers. You will hear a voice in you insist that it does not want to suffer, but we quickly discover that is not so when we try to end the suffering. How do we end the suffering?

Decide to meditate.

Choose to do attention/awareness exercises.

Plan regular silent retreats.

Commit to a sitting group.

Let go of a habit.

Then watch how resistance arises. Listen to the internal voices telling you, "No, you don't want to do that." "All I'm doing is helping you not to suffer," they explain. But you will never end the suffering of egocentricity. Egocentricity is suffering.

The only way to end suffering is to see through the process that keeps us believing in our separateness from all that is. Now, each time we see through a piece of that process, each time we step beyond the mistaken view we've been conditioned to believe in, those same voices—the voices of egocentric conditioning—will tell us we are wrong or stupid or worse. Having a chance to say out loud what we hear from those voices is a powerful way of disengaging from them. And that is one of the things I treasure about doing awareness practice with others. Things that sound unquestionably true inside our heads become less convincing when we say them aloud.

I would encourage you to do all the exercises in the book, and to pay close attention to your reactions to the exercises, whatever they may be. Each exercise is followed by a discussion, consisting of a sample of questions and comments from people in the online workshop, along with my responses. By participating fully in this process as you go through this book, you can prove to yourself that suffering is optional.

Contents

Ending suffering requires us to see how suffering happens.
If we are willing to be quiet and pay attention to the process of
suffering, every moment of life becomes an opportunity to step
beyond illusion into freedom.

We all hold untold numbers of beliefs about ourselves, others,
and life in general, and we operate out of those beliefs
unconsciously. Examining our beliefs, dropping them, and returning
attention to the present is essential to ending suffering.

It is possible to end suffering by living in the awareness that
nothing in the universe is personal. But we are taught to take
life very personally, and we feel like "a someone" to whom "life
is happening." But this is an illusion. By paying attention and
believing nothing, we can dispel the illusion.

The First Key

Pay
attention
to
everything

OUR EXPERIENCE of life is determined by the focus of our attention. The person whose attention is focused on what is wrong lives in a sea of imperfection. Focusing on lack creates a life of deprivation. Focusing on violence creates fear of danger.

Understanding that this is so has inspired "the power of positive thinking," "daily affirmations," and a whole host of attempts to control the content of our minds. "Having a positive attitude" and "looking on the bright side" are offered as ways to address the recognition that what we attend to determines the quality of our lives.

I am not a fan of positive thinking and affirmations for two main reasons.

1. The powerful forces of our conditioning are just as opposed to a positive outlook as to a negative one. We are bounced back and forth from one extreme to another, which produces constant dissatisfaction. When we're on the negative side, we want the positive; when we have the positive, we want to keep it, but because it is the nature of life to change, we cannot, and we are tossed back to the negative side. The world of duality, in which everything is either/or, good/bad, right/wrong, desirable/undesirable, has no place for satisfaction, contentment, ease.

2. Positive and negative are both content, not process, and attending to how processes work is much more helpful than trying to change a particular piece of content. For example, rather than assume I need to change myself or the world before I can stop worrying (or being afraid or jealous or filled with regret or whatever the form of suffering), it is more effective to address the process of worrying. I do this by attending to
  what worry is,
   how it works,
     where it comes from,
       what purpose it serves in my life,
        what I believe about it,
          how my life is with worry in it,
            and how my life might be without worry.

All we need to do is pay attention. We don't have to decide if something is good or bad, right or wrong.

We don't need to have judgments about what kind of person we are because we have certain kinds of thoughts or feelings or reactions. That is the road to suffering. Our job is quite different:

Just notice.

What is actually happening, right now?

We notice this,
then this,
then that,
then that. . .

We pay attention to all of it.
Where is the suffering?

BY CONCENTRATING on the process of attention, how attention works and how it is related to awareness, we can see the difference between consciously paying attention and our habitual conditioned attention. A big part of the process of suffering is the fact that before we bring conscious awareness to life, ego/conditioning is in control of the focus of our attention.

When we attempt to wake up from delusion, to bring focus to attention, to live in conscious awareness, ego goes into overdrive to stop us. Once we are paying close attention to our experience, we may notice fear arising. Ego does not like to be scrutinized, and it has many ways of keeping us from scrutinizing it. Those ways are the content of our awareness practice, the issues we work with. We forget, fall asleep, get distracted, feel bored, doubt ourselves, believe we are inadequate, discover something else that has to be done now, feel afraid--all tools egocentricity uses to keep control of the lives that would otherwise be ours to live in freedom and ease.

We can learn to pay attention to something like fear

4

with a completely neutral attitude of curiosity, even fascination. We sit still and simply watch sensations arise in the body,
thoughts attach to the sensations,
emotions attach to the thoughts,
beliefs attach to the emotions,
and behaviors attach to the beliefs.

Then an amazing, miraculous thing happens:
We can see that none of it means anything!
(This experience is often followed by
a great knee-slapping laugh.)

So stay with it. Don't let fear scare you off. As it says in our <u>Fear</u> <u>Book</u>, fear is a green light that signals you're on the right track and need to put the pedal to the metal.

Here is what I asked the class to do:

Sit in a quiet place. Close your eyes if that feels comfortable, and allow your breath to deepen. Long, slow, relaxed breaths. Not forcing anything, just gradually letting the breath become more relaxed and easy. Picture that the breath is serving as awareness. As you take a breath in, allow your awareness to expand with the breath until your whole body is filled with breath and awareness. As you exhale, feel your navel draw in toward your spine as the breath leaves your body. All of your awareness is with the navel pulling toward the spine. Inhale, and feel your body expand with the breath. Feel the breath and the awareness of the breath filling your whole body down into your fingers and toes. Practice this for several breaths.

In this process you are becoming familiar with a field of awareness. The attention is not moving from thing to thing to thing as is its habit, but instead is relaxing into the awareness. The feeling is quite similar to allowing the eyes to go out of focus. For just a moment or so, let your vision rest several feet out in front of you. Move your eyes slowly around the scene in front of you to take in as much as you can of what is in your view. Move your eyes from object to object, noticing colors, textures, and shapes.

Now, let your eyes go out of focus. You are still seeing, but you are not seeing any one thing in particular. There is a scene, a view, but you are not looking at any particular object or shape or color. You can bring one thing into view by focusing on that thing. For a moment or so practice that movement: in focus, out of focus. Can you feel the expansion and contraction? Can you follow the movement of your attention during this process? Attention is on the out of focus expansive view, then it moves to one particular object. Your eyes go out of focus and your attention turns toward the out of focus view. Turn your attention to one thing and your eyes bring that object into focus.

Now, let's go back to the breath, feeling the awareness of the breath as the breath fills the whole body. As you exhale, feel the breath leave the body and allow the awareness to follow the breath as the breath leaves the body--same relaxed lack of focus, awareness expanding to include everything in the range of your sight and hearing, focusing on nothing in particular, but aware of everything in an undifferentiated way. Practice this for several breaths.

Can you sense that your attention is focused on your awareness? Try several more breaths with that in mind: Your attention is focused on awareness as awareness moves with the breath. Awareness is with the breath as you inhale, you're aware of your body expanding as you take in the air, you can feel your whole body expanding at the same time because attention is on awareness rather than having to move from thing to thing in order to give you the information that your body is expanding with the inhalation.

This is a very important step and I want to be sure everyone is being able to sense these movements. We are practicing being aware of attention moving in the field of awareness. Attention moves to something in particular and that is what we are aware of. My attention focuses on the baby crying and I am aware of the baby crying. My attention moves to the people laughing, and for a moment I do not hear the baby crying as my awareness consists of the people laughing. My attention moves to a memory of me laughing with people I love. The people in front of me, the crying baby, disappear as my awareness is taken up with the memory. I remember to look to see what my attention is doing. Awareness focuses on attention. Attention is attending to awareness. There's a sound and my attention goes to the sound. Do I go with the attention and get lost in the sound, or am I aware of attention going to the sound and remain aware of the movements of attention...

Remember: This is awareness practice and you cannot do it wrong.

Responses

This exercise gave me some anxiety, because even though you said we couldn't do it wrong, I knew I couldn't do it just as you described. Especially the part about attention being on awareness. I'm not able to experience that.

Not able to experience it, <u>yet</u>.
Fortunately, we get more than one chance. In fact, if the Buddha was right, there is life after life after life in which to practice. This is not a contest, it is awareness practice. We get to do it over and over again, and when we get to a place where we are pretty sure this is IT, nothing will change except we will enjoy practicing even more.

I understand about dropping the thought and coming back to the breath and not getting caught up in the internal dramas, but I have trouble doing that while accomplishing tasks, interacting with another person, and especially making decisions and knowing when to speak up or take action. I know I keep going to my head, and feelings of fear usually sabotage me. After years of working with all this and much searching, I find some clarity, then I seem to get stuck in the suffering again, and I feel overwhelmed and helpless.

I think you know that the suffering lives in your head. Now the work is to practice what you know.
The internal voices are so insistent: "But what about...?" You hesitate, you feel confused. "Well, maybe they're right. What about...? Shouldn't I figure it out?"

Here is the deal: There is nothing wrong with "going to your head," which usually means looking to egocentric conditioning to tell you what to do. However, as long as you allow that conditioning to guide your life, you will suffer. I wish I had another answer. But only when you reach the point of not caring a fig about the "yeah buts" or the "what abouts" will you be free. That need to go up into the head to check in with conditioning about your life is the source of your feeling overwhelmed and hopeless.

Now for the good news: All you need to do to have

all that misery fall away is to stay with your attention as it focuses in this moment. I can hear people snorting, "Did she say ALL?" But I can promise you that staying present is a piece of cake in comparison to living in the agony of egocentric conditioning.

The exercise threw me. My mind/ego acts like a child with ADHD [attention deficit hyperactivity disorder]: I focus my attention, and in a flash I feel drowsy, or a voice says, "You can't do this," "This is really boring," and the like. I try to take that ADHD child/ego by the hand and kindly placate it, but it's very strong.

And you will be very strong by the time you make peace with this "child." Yes, this is boring, this is stupid, you don't want to do it, you want to do something else—on and on ego drones. At least it is honest. The "I" DOES feel drowsy, the "I" IS bored, the "I" CAN'T do it. Just don't get confused about who you are and who it is. You are the one who CAN do it.

Oh, and by the way, if you are meditating, you're good at it. Every meditation is a good meditation.

Don't let egocentricity critique you. The only bad meditation is the one you don't do.

I have been in physical pain for the past couple of years, and it takes all I can do to distract myself from the pain so I can cope with life. When I try to bring my attention to my body and the present moment, my awareness is of the pain. How does one do this work in the midst of physical pain?

That is the crux of the matter, isn't it? I would take the "physical" out of it, though, and ask "How does one do this work in the midst of pain?" You have identified the entire point of this practice: Pain is inevitable; suffering is optional.

Egocentricity has a field day with pain, doesn't it? How does ego take advantage of your pain? It says, "This pain is real. You have to do, say, feel, and behave the way conditioning tells you, because this pain is REAL! You can't meditate, you can't be present, you have to live in distraction, because there is pain when you are present with life." How handy for a system that has its life "outside the present," in an illusion of separation from life.

I offer this to you as an alternative. It's not an

easy alternative, but remember that living in distraction from life in order to avoid pain is not easy either. Imagine that you have a child, whom you love utterly, who has the kind of pain you have. There is nothing you can do to take the pain away from this child you adore. All of your love cannot save this child. What can you do? You can be with that child. You can hold that child and say, "I cannot take this pain from you, but I will be  with you. I will stay right here, loving you, treasuring you, and I will do whatever I can to help you be as happy as you can be. I will help you explore the pain and see if we can lessen it. I will help you see what you can do in spite of the pain. I will cheer your victories and weep at your struggles and love you more every day."

Pain is inevitable. With conscious, compassionate, loving acceptance and care, suffering is not an option we ever need to entertain.

IN BUDDHISM if there were an "original sin," it would be assumption. Assumption is the veil of ignorance that keeps us from seeing what is, and failure to see what is leads us to suffering. We don't pay attention to what we assume to be so, and we don't even notice that we are not paying attention.

Our most basic assumption is that we are the way we see ourselves and the world is the way we see it. We are taught to believe life should be a certain way and we should be a certain way. When it isn't and we aren't, we assume there's something wrong and something should be done to fix things. Suffering happens when we want life to be other than the way it is.

This belief in "life as it should be" often leads to self-judgment and attempts at self-improvement. Neither of these activities is helpful. In this practice, we turn away from assumptions that something is wrong with us or with life and from the self-criticism that results, and we begin to dismantle the processes that keep these erroneous views in place.

Suffering is a habit of thought, emotion, perception, and interpretation. We continue to see the same things as long as we look to the same assumptions in the same way. But we can learn to recognize and question our assumptions, explore what we habitually attend to and ignore, and see our beliefs as the conditioned opinions they are rather than the "truth" we have been taught to believe them to be.

Most important of all, we will come to understand that none of this is our "fault." We are not to blame for life. No one needs to be blamed, because in fact there is nothing wrong with life or with us. When we see through our false views, we realize that, exactly as it is, life is perfect.

Here is what I asked the class to do:

Notice at least one assumption you make. An excellent way to recognize assumptions is to ask "How do I know that?" when you are speaking or acting from a place of "knowing" or "certainty."

Remember, this is awareness practice. You cannot do it wrong. Just pay attention to every thought, feeling and conditioned assumption as you go through the day--everything you notice (even judgment) informs you.

Responses

My immediate assumption when I read the exercise was "I know all this already, I don't need to do this course." And I drifted away from doing the work because I bought into that assumption.

When we hear the equivalent of "I already know this," we can "know" several things: 1) we don't know, 2) ego is threatened, and 3) this is a very good thing to be doing because we just got a glimpse of our conditioning. Knowing prevents seeing. We cannot simultaneously hold on to something from the past and be here,

fresh and open,

in this moment.

Things I assume:
I would be happier if I were married.
If I had more money, I would feel safer.
Life would be easier if I had grown up in a loving home.
I will always have trouble trusting people.
A lot of assumptions—not sure what to do with them.

There is nothing to do with these assumptions,
except to note that they arise. "Doing" is the
lifeblood of egocentric conditioning. Every time we
have a profound awareness, every time we get close
to seeing through a process of our conditioning that
keeps us stuck where we are, the voices are going
to come up with some form of doing. "What should
I do? How do I deal with this?
How can I get rid of this?"

There is nothing to do. Just sit,
breathe, relax. Awareness
expands to include everything.
Attention rests quietly in awareness. And when you
are paying attention, everything enlightens you.

I received a large tax return, and I'm worried that something will
go wrong to take it all (car breaking down, a large bill or

something). I am asking myself where this fear came from and why I believe it. It seems like a self-fulfilling prophecy.

Notice how you get pulled away into thinking about things like fear and self-fulfilling prophecies. When the urge to figure things out arises, you can just notice that. Then, move the attention back to the breath. Attention on the breath, on awareness. Awareness relaxing to include all. "But what about the money?" Just notice, then back to the breath.

I am having trouble with the concept that suffering is optional, that life is perfect. If that is so, then it seems as if the obvious thing for a person to do in regard to other suffering beings is nothing—because it is only their assumptions that create the suffering. For people whose basic needs are taken care of, I can see that much suffering we bring to ourselves simply by wanting things to be different. However, in developing countries where HIV/AIDS and TB are rampant and lead to a slow and painful death; where mothers lose children to malaria, malnutrition, tetanus; where there are no pain medications for persons with broken limbs, is suffering optional?

This may sound hard-hearted, but this kind of response is what egocentric conditioning does to throw us completely off the track. We're not talking about any of those things here. Do they exist? Of course they exist. The whole point of what the Buddha taught is that 1) life is suffering, 2) suffering has a cause, 3) ending suffering is possible, and 4) there is a way to do that. What we are doing is learning the way to end suffering. If we keep focused on its existence, one thing I can promise you: Suffering will never end.

Here is a big hint. Conditioning is always going to try to pull you up into your head, into your conditioned reality, as a way to take you out of this moment, away from here/now. Just notice that and try not to fall for it. Be aware of how easy it is to get lost in the story. We can be noticing assumption, and suddenly the attention is completely lost in the "content" of the assumption.

Again, it is helpful if we stay here. A big tool of egocentric karmic conditioning is "let's go over there and think about that," and before you know it, you're mired in a world of suffering. Insight (which is the process of seeing) does not require thinking. Thinking simply takes us away from where insight happens.

My assumptions today:
I am bound to be a failure in love,
in work, in life in general.
Everything "bad" that happens is
evidence that I am doomed to
failure.
My loserness is inherent in me.
I should just give up.

Putting these thoughts into words makes them seem absurd.
However, they carry such power that even when I've seen
through them, the same assumptions keep coming back. That
kind of persistence would serve me well if harnessed. I wonder
if it is possible to transform this into something more
supportive?

I wonder if it is possible to lose interest in it and
let it go. While we are rumbling around in our
heads, lost in conditioned thought, the moments slide
by unnoticed. Remember, the quality of our life is
determined by the focus of our attention. The
lightning-fast movement of attention from thing to
thing makes it appear that it can "multi-task," but
that is not so. Attention is strictly on one thing at
a time. It is not possible to have full attention on,
say, the breath, and simultaneously maintain self-
hating diatribes.

Notice how conditioning resists the simple practice of paying attention to the breath. Notice the thoughts about it, then bring attention back to the breath. The attention wanders; bring it back to the breath. Frustration arises; back to the breath. Can it be a game? Can you let it be fun?

The assumption that causes me the most suffering is that I want to be with my fiancé forever, and that he is going to leave me, I'm not good enough, and I will be lonely the rest of my life, no matter what I do. I am learning to watch the process as I fall into that assumption and see what happens. But I still tend to get stuck in listening to the voices.

Yes! And right there is the suffering, isn't it? The voices start telling you what is so, and you have a habit of listening to them. Like a child with an old, familiar lullaby, we get lulled in to a sleepy state by the voices. "He's going to leave. You're not good enough. He's so wonderful, why would he stay with you?" We become mesmerized, hypnotized by the familiar refrain. Deeper and deeper we plunge into misery.

That is precisely why we are training ourselves not to allow our attention to go off by itself. When it goes off without us, it goes into unsavory places, and we wind up in hell. Right now we are learning to recognize that habit. We are watching to see what assumptions lure us away from conscious awareness, which conditioned patterns pull our attention into that world of suffering.

This may not be comforting right now, but you can learn to use that misery as a flag to bring you back to conscious awareness. Those voices will begin to signal you to be <u>here</u>. Sounds like you already have a good start.

I love the experience of having an understanding come and go. I can tell when I'm seeing something from pretty close to "center," that is, free of conditioned thoughts and feelings. Then it is simply clear and makes powerful sense. When I am seeing something through the perspective of my conditioning, I can't seem to understand it at all. That experience of being at center (clear) and being in conditioning (confused) is very useful, because we can go back and forth until we recognize each state, the movement between them, and how to get from confused to clear.

I notice the assumption that although I have been practicing paying attention for a while, I can't make it work. I feel stuck. Then there is another voice that says, "You have special powers of insight. You can do this really well." My mind is terribly contradictory.

The trick is to turn the attention on this "I" who has been doing the practice for a while, who can't make it work, who feels stuck, who listens to the voices, who says you have special powers of insight, who believes what the voices say. There really is no contradiction; there is one "I," one illusion of a separate self who is calling all the shots, and that is the only problem.

 We are a quick-fix, instant-gratification-is-too-slow society, but the reality is that this takes practice. It took us a while to get trained to these faulty belief systems, and it will take us a while to unhook ourselves. We sit still, we see the conditioning and the sabotage for what it is, and we find the courage not to go back to old, familiar, hurtful ways.

I'm reading this assignment again this morning and feeling anxiety and confusion, thinking, "I don't know what this means!"

"I don't know"--what a delicious place to be if you have been bitten by the bug of awareness! Keep looking. And here is my hope and prayer for you: May you never know, may you never stop paying attention!

The ultimate weapon against the torture of egocentric conditioning is tenacity, perseverance, downright stubbornness. Just keep on plugging along, one foot in front of the other. If you can, throw in a dose of "I'm just grateful to know there is a possibility of finding my way out of this suffering." When you have a moment of clarity (and you know you do, even though ego would like you to believe you don't), say a big thank you to everything in you that is willing and sincere.

"HABIT" IS another area that fosters ignorance and delusion and hides a great deal of our suffering. When we act out of habit and are not aware we are doing so, suffering is often the result.

Here is what I asked the class to do:

Sit back, allow your eyes to go slightly out of focus, turn your attention to your breath, and take ten long, slow, easy breaths.

At the end of ten breaths, turn your attention to your experience of "habit."

What feelings does the word "habit" stir in you?

In what ways are habits good?

How do habits support you?

How are habits negative?

Are you a "habit" kind of person?

What habits have you been unable to break?

What habits have you successfully broken?

Are there things you "just can't live without?" Of the things you "can't live without," do you consider some positive and some negative?

What is the relationship between preferences and habits?

Throughout your day keep "habit" at the front of your conscious awareness. Notice your habits. Notice other people's habits. Do we, as a society, have shared habits? How do we feel about one another's habits? Do you have different language for your habits and other people's habits? Notice everything you can about habit.

And don't forget to pay attention to how you approach this assignment, to bring conscious awareness to the process.

Responses

As soon as I sit back, settle down, and think "habit," my mind goes off in several directions, none leading anywhere but confusion.

Confusion--along with being tired, overwhelmed, fearful, bored, burdened--is one of the little tricks ego plays to keep us from awareness of what conditioning is doing with our lives. Here's a trick you can use in return: Focus all of your attention on confusion. Watch closely. Forget about trying to be clear, just notice everything you can about confusion. Turn the tables on it!

Egocentricity is always going to feel overwhelmed and discouraged when we look at it. Because we are so accustomed to thinking of it as us, when it feels something, we think it _is_ us. It takes a good deal of looking to sense the difference between those two perspectives, egocentric conditioning, on the one hand, and on the other, a larger, more centered perspective—that of authenticity, or true nature, authentic self, essence, that which animates. Egocentricity says, "I am seeing this," wanting there to be only one self. But there isn't, and the discouragement you feel is ego trying to get you to give up looking at it. But don't quit! The confusion itself is a sign that you're onto something, and ego knows it.

I seem to use habits to support a rigid notion of myself and the world, in an effort to make it more manageable. However, once I am operating from a habit, I am less likely to be fully engaged in what I am doing, because I am on "autopilot." It seems as if I try to constantly establish habits so I can "check out."

Yes, indeed. And who would want to check out rather than be here for life? Egocentric, karmic conditioning, which has its life in the past and future and does not, cannot, exist in the present.

At first thought, habits seem to me to be positive. I am an opera singer, and vocal technique is basically a set of habits, automatizing your responses, in a sense. I find this helpful and reassuring, so I would say this habit supports me.

We are conditioned to believe that habits are positive and negative, but that's just conditioning. I do not believe any activity requires habit or is benefited by habit. Singing is a perfect example. I can learn to hold my body in a particular way and breathe in a particular way to make a certain sound with my voice. I practice that so I can produce notes called for by the music. I don't practice a note so I can go unconscious and not be present to singing that note! My voice learns how to produce that particular sound, and conscious awareness and attention keep the process fresh and new.

Is that saying we shouldn't have habits? No. What makes the difference is whether or not we are consciously present in the moment. I'm not interested in whether people have "bad" habits that they should break and are "good" people for breaking them. I just want us to know what habit is and what it does in our lives. Here is an outrageous statement: I would rather know what smoking is and does in my life—what needs it fulfills, where judgments about it come from, how I can see through those judgments and let them go—than quit smoking. Most important to me is to realize how I can be free in any circumstance.

There is no freedom in focusing on getting it right. In the end, we may or may not meet anyone's standards of "right" (including our own), but if we can see beyond and live beyond the illusions of a dualistic reality, we will be free. I, for one, would far prefer to be free than to be right.

I have OCD (obsessive/compulsive disorder), and I therefore assume that the intrusive urge of "having" to perform my habits over and over ad nauseum brings me more suffering than any one else. It is so difficult to find any equanimity and compassion and lovingkindness when I think about how my brain malfunctions. I wish I could have a new brain, but people with diabetes probably wish they could have a new pancreas.

Good for you! What a difficult illusion to see through. Our karma always wants us to believe that it is the worst, has the worst deal, is the most put-upon. You are so right—the person with diabetes could think OCD a piece of cake. The person in poverty can believe that money would solve all problems. It is so easy for us to fall for the "I have it so bad that I need X to make up for it," and the karmic beat goes on. In your awareness, there is something for all of us to apply. When we see that life is a struggle for everyone, we can share the attitude Ram Dass described: Life is so difficult, how can we not hold hands as we approach it?

I keep hoping for a magic solution to what I call the habit of "I hate you." The frustrating part is that "it" is me!

The good news is that "it" is not "you" in the sense of who you really are. Self-hate is like a parasite that lives in you, but it is not you. I like the notion of seeing it as a habit. When you are conscious and paying attention, it has no access to you. But when your attention drifts off for even a moment. . .boom, there it is and it has you. It steals your time, your joy, your good feeling about yourself. It steals your life.

Have you done our "There Is Nothing Wrong With You" retreat? It is designed specifically to address this particularly nasty habit of self-hate. I would encourage anyone struggling with the "I hate you" habit to give that work a chance.

Consider what life would be like if you didn't feel bad about being the way you are. Just imagine the opening, the potential, the possibility. Awareness is the most exciting thing there is when self-hate doesn't take charge of it. In just noticing, the old falls away and the new is revealed, bright and shiny.

When I notice that I am "really being aware," the thought is, "See, I can be nice and focused." So rather than just being me, I'm pretending to be me being nice and focused. This habit—a habit because it keeps coming up—is the kind I struggle with. What I really want is to be genuinely me, but it sure is tough to get past all of the habit-energy!

It is tough, and that's why relaxation is the only way to approach it. Just breathing and relaxing and noticing, feeling that what is genuinely you breathes and relaxes and notices.

I felt a bit overwhelmed by this discussion. The excitement about exploring and learning something new is quickly squashed by the fear of not measuring up to the standards that I be brilliant, profound, the best. "Make sure you do really well on this assignment about noticing habits! You better come up with some breakthrough insights." Self-hate pushes me to participate then tells me how excruciatingly high the standards are and how lame my thoughts are. Then I give in to resistance; I procrastinate about sitting down with the assignment, I put off responding. But laying the process out like this feels satisfying. It's self-hate that is exposed.

Yes, yes, yes. We do this to reveal that which is ruining our lives, this miserable, fiendish self-hating habit. However, knowing that doesn't make it feel any better when it's revealed, and that's why we keep at it. We reveal it, we feel awful, but we see the process. We look deeper, something else is revealed, we feel awful. Soon we become familiar with the process and start taking the whole thing less personally. We read other people's responses and begin to see that we are not as alone in this as we had thought. After a while the voices kick in, and our response is, "Oh, yeah, the voices again."

The most devastating habit for me is guilt. Every memory conjures up something to feel guilty about, and waves of morose feelings envelop me. When I am in the middle of that cycle, it is all consuming and all pervasive and has the tenacity of an outraged pit bull. Am I on the right track to consider this just a habit? It seems a lot more powerful than that.

Here is my best encouragement when working with something that has as much power in your life as guilt has. Continue with the work that we're doing, but make guilt the focus of all the work. In other words, what habits support guilt? What do you assume about guilt? Where do you focus your attention to experience guilt? What does guilt mean? Where do you feel it? What does having guilt keep you from facing? Turn the spotlight of awareness on the subject of guilt. Look at it from every angle, up and down, inside and out. You be the pit bull—grab hold of guilt and don't turn loose until you are the world's foremost expert on the subject. Write the book on guilt!

THIS EXERCISE continues our exploration of habits.

Here is what I asked the class to do:

Take ten long, deep, relaxed breaths, allowing all of your attention to focus on your breathing. As you breathe, see if you can let go of everything other than breathing in and breathing out.

As part of your exploration of the subject of habit and your relationship with it, make a list of your habits. Take as much time as you need.

Now, review the list you made of your personal habits. Choose three to work with for this exercise, and write them down, one for each of the next three days.

The exercise is to break the habit consciously, attentively, and mindfully.

Take a moment or so to consider how you will do that. Will you not smoke? Will you drink tea instead of coffee? Will you take a different route to work? Will you not watch TV? Will you listen to a different type of music? Give yourself as much time as you need to decide how you will go about altering your relationship with this particular piece of life "content." If it would be helpful, write down your plan of attack. How will you remember to break the habit? Will you need props or reminders or support? How might you arrange that?

Pay close attention to everything about this process you are participating in.

Responses

For weeks, my neighbor's yappy little dog has been barking. Today I was particularly angry because their cat had cried outside my window all night. I got mad and almost said a few things in anger. Instead, when the dog started barking again tonight, I just listened to the barking, breathing and listening, without attaching my feelings about it. The actual sound of the barking is not that bad, if I focus on it alone. It's when I start in about how this might go on forever and how inconsiderate it is for people to let their dogs and cats disturb their neighbors and how in a perfect world there wouldn't be any barking dogs and crying cats and on and on. It was a relief to let go of all that!

I have a friend who says when shoveling snow or running to catch a bus, "Don't you love it when fitness pays off in practical ways?" I love it when awareness pays off in practical ways. I can either lie in bed feeling miserable and hating life because a dog or a cat is enjoying its life, or I can just attend to my awareness, be aware of awareness, and enjoy being alive.

I brushed and flossed my teeth last night for what felt like the very first time. I started flossing at the bottom right of my mouth instead of the top left. I had to pay extra attention or I would lose track of where I was. I felt the pressure applied between my teeth and against my gums. I saw each individual tooth and watched how my tongue followed the floss around. In the mirror I saw the funny faces I was making. I felt the tingle of the toothpaste against my tongue, marveling at the incredible experience of having all this sensation and flavor in my mouth. Who has been brushing and flossing my teeth all these years? I am so excited that I get to apply this process to all the things I have been doing but not paying attention to. Next stop— scrubbing the kitchen floor.

The spiritual life is just one long fun-filled romp, isn't it? We can chuckle about that, but we also have to acknowledge that it is true. In this practice, an expression we use constantly is, "It's not what, it's how." Finding that kind of delight in brushing the teeth is exactly what is meant. We are conditioned to believe that life has to be a certain way for us to enjoy it. We are trained to live for the big moments, the special events, the times that are inherently enjoyable. What we find with practice, though, is that every moment to which we are present is joyful. Presence itself is joy-full; the content is irrelevant.

I am teaching my eight-year-old daughter to cook. I asked her to get the eggs out as the first step in making an omelet. To my astonishment, she removed three eggs randomly from the carton.

She has no idea that there is a "way" to do this. My way, my life-long habit (where did I learn it?) is to remove eggs from the carton consecutively, in rows. In the space of thirty seconds, I felt shocked by my daughter's simple random choice, appreciative of its beauty (the pattern in the carton is lovely), and amazed that I think there is a "right way" to take eggs out of a carton. I never think about this habit, but I do it the same way, unconsciously, always.

I did not "correct" the egg pattern or discuss my revelation. My delight in this discovery stayed with me all day, and I would catch myself smiling about it often. In this shift in awareness about habits, I find myself paying attention to what habits I am teaching my daughter—and to what she is teaching me.

What a marvelous opportunity! When you read "enlightenment stories" from any tradition, the experience you describe is the common element. Someone, an acknowledged or accidental "master" (someone who is not operating out of karmic conditioning) is present to a situation in a fresh, spontaneous way. In that person's response, those sharing the circumstance are catapulted into that fresh moment along with the "master." It is even possible to read about it later and be catapulted into that "Ah!" with an eyes-wide-open response. In a split second, the whole known world turns upside down and inside out. We are left breathless and delightfully shaken.

FOR ME, the following participant response articulated perfectly what we are up against with our habits. As a matter of fact, it leads us to our next area of focus.

Thank you for this exercise. It helps me see that I do almost everything exactly the same way every day. I feel disoriented and confused whenever I vary my routines. I find that my habits are comforting. They give me the illusion of predictability and control, which seems like safety. They also protect me from feeling overwhelmed and over stimulated by the incredible array of options in each moment. My habits mean I don't have to consciously choose anything, and I then avoid the stress of making choices and decisions.

I don't have to worry about making a "poor" choice as I think I know where each well-worn path will lead me. This illusion of predictability is very important to me, as it helps me feel that I'm in a safe corner of a profoundly unpredictable and unsafe feeling world. I made a very long list of my daily habits, and find that the thought of changing any of them is quite frightening. I'm worried that I'll forget something "important," e.g. to take my medications, or something I need for work, if I vary my morning ritual. If I shower and dress before breakfast, I worry that I'll spill oat bran on my work clothes, which seems silly as I write it, and still too scary to try. I've spent quite a while this evening trying to find any of my habits that I'd feel comfortable changing tomorrow, and each one feels crucial. Even a little thing like brushing my teeth after rather than before my morning shower feels risky somehow. I have no idea what I'd actually risk by doing that, though. There's a lot going on with this exercise for me. I'm curious to see how this unfolds.

Here is what I asked the class to do:

Pay attention to <u>control</u> for a whole day. Notice your feelings and experiences related to control, and to write down what you feel you can and cannot control.

Responses

Control, to me, is a negative word. It connotes a desire to have power over someone or something. After this assignment, I see my need to control in many things I do or say, even if those things seem passive. Lately I've been seeking to control my emotions, especially sadness over the end of a relationship. After finally realizing that I cannot control how someone else reacts to me, I turned that desire to control back toward myself. Sometimes it works, but most of the time the emotions have to have their say.

The control we think we have is the control egocentricity has over us. "You need to control your emotions!" conditioning says to us, and we believe it. Can we control our emotions? No, although we can depress them. But our lives are dictated by our attempts to do what conditioning tells us to do. The voice that says, "You should have control" controls us utterly.

Conditioning controls us by convincing us that without its control, we would be dangerous, horrible. We must prove to ourselves that without conditioning controlling us, we would in fact be kinder, gentler, more loving and compassionate (not to mention creative, brilliant, happy, excited, and enthusiastic) than we would ever have believed possible. The only way to prove that to ourselves is to step free of the conditioning and see what is there when it is not.

We have no control over what we get in life, but we can learn to have every choice about how we respond. Choice is available to us when we let go of the illusion of control.

I feel I have control over my choices. I can choose to review a document before a meeting, or I can choose not to. That feels comfortable to me. My body relaxes with the knowledge that in this moment I have control through my choice.

With the "do have control over" items, is it <u>control</u>, as in, "I am in charge of this and can make it happen any time, anywhere," or is it <u>choice</u>, as in, "I can bring conscious, compassionate awareness to this area and have a good chance of affecting the outcome in a direction that leads away from suffering"? A lot of people hit their control issues like a brick wall when they develop insomnia, others when they decide to begin a meditation practice and their conditioning won't let them sit. Again, there's no control, but there is choice, even in the most difficult situations that life presents.

When I first read the exercise it seemed clear to me that I can control my reactions, my thoughts, what I feel, but as the day unfolded, I became less sure. I was hurt by another person, and my feelings seemed to go "out of control." By last night, I thought, "I feel what I feel, and I felt hurt. I didn't need to control my feelings to feel something different that I thought was more right." I've spent my entire life trying to be in control, which for me was blocking out feelings. The last year I began to feel, and I seemed "out of control." As I write this email, I'm becoming more confused.

The process you describe is so important for all of us to see through. You write a perfectly clear, articulate description of what happened to you, and at the end you are left confused. How did that happen? What you described was not confusing. You realized that conditioning wanted you to control your emotions so you wouldn't simply be able to feel what you feel. What is confusing about that? My answer is, nothing. But your realization is so threatening  to ego that it has to sprinkle you with Stupid Dust (as we call it around the monastery). Egocentricity sees that you have reached a point of clarity and flies into action, zooming up to the top of your head and, poof, a little cloud of Stupid Dust envelopes you. Suddenly you can't remember anything. "What insight? Having emotion is all right? I don't understand. . ."

Do you see how that works? You have come to the intelligent awareness that feeling emotions does not signal that a person is "out of control." But, fear of being out of control is the primary threat conditioning uses to control us. Ego tells us, "If you feel your feelings, you will act on them, and then god knows what might happen. Don't feel anything! Control yourself, and I (oh, no, I meant to say "you") will be fine. Here, I will control you to be sure you control yourself, and we'll both be fine." Don't fall for it! We spend our lives in torment, trying to avoid feeling emotions that, if we allowed them, would last a matter of moments. The awareness that we do not need to control our emotions is vital.

Today the first habit on my list of habits (always expecting the worst) met control (lack of) head on. Within half an hour, I learned that my husband has hepatitis and a lifelong special friend has stomach cancer. No control. And I saw how immediately I expected the worst in both cases. Why not expect the good? Who tells me that all will be negative? It's a dark belief I've lived with all my life, but I see it now, and I'm going to start looking at that negativity from every angle.

To live as you suggest from that attitude of "How do I know that?" can open up so many possibilities. There's "I'm sure it will be horrible/I'm sure it will be fine," and then there's just "I really don't know." It is possible to be with ourselves in an attitude of compassionate acceptance regardless of the circumstances. It takes practice. When life is so challenging, the need for compassionate acceptance is apparent, but we still need to be patient with our lack of practice. You've had an awareness that I suspect will make your life a lot easier, but that habit of looking toward the bleak outcome is old and deep and tenacious. Please be gentle with yourself as you let go of an approach to life that has seemed for so long to <u>be</u> you.

I thought about control when I was looking at a cartoon that shows a man standing at a crossroads, with signs pointing in each direction. One sign says "Your wildest dreams come true," and the other says, "Someone more interesting's wildest dreams come true." It raises the question, what kind of person are you to want what you want? I think I want to trust my own decisions for my life. I can't control how things turn out, but I'd rather know that

I'm living by my dreams and not someone else's.

As long as you are a person who does regret or doubt, there will always be something to doubt or regret, just as the person who does anger always finds something to be angry about and the person who does guilt always has something to feel guilty about. The content is irrelevant. If the attachment to a particular process is great enough, we can simply make up some content to fit it; that is, a guilty person will fabricate sins to feel bad about. Trying to resolve life's problems via content will take you around in circles. If, however, you resolve the process, it does not matter where you go or what you do, you will just be there doing that. There is no parallel universe in which you have the life you should have had. There is only the life you have, and most people miss their lives because they allow egocentricity to trade what is for what "should" be.

The major control issue in my life involves the belief that if I work hard and discipline myself I can control the outcome and be successful in my profession and in my life in general. Consequently, my response to adversity has always been to work harder and deny myself fun things and leisure periods.

Though I feel this belief system is faulty, it is hard for me to get to its roots and dissolve it. After all, I have been exposed to this doctrine through my education and am relentlessly confronted with it in my job. A number of years ago, I experienced a professional failure which I could not "control" (meaning solve) although I was working like a maniac. That left me depressed, and I still carry a bit of the depression with me. I find it hard to do good work without inherently trying to control the outcome, and I realized recently (in part through this assignment) that it keeps me away from happiness and is something I need to work on.

That is the huge reality that we must all face sooner or later (and I support sooner): You can seem to control things until you can't. People take their health for granted until they lose it. We take loved ones for granted until we lose them. We think we're going to be young forever until we get old. We can hear from the healthy that we should be able to heal ourselves if we have enough faith and think positively--a great theory unless you're one of the ones for whom it doesn't work.

What is required is a peaceful sit-in against the voices of conditioning that control you. Your attitude can be, "No, I am not going to do that. No, I am not going to respond to that pressure." When you try it the first time, it will feel as if the voices are going to kill you. But they can't. Sit still and there is nothing that can happen to you. All your nerve endings will feel as if they're coming through your skin, but they aren't. When it's all over, you'll get to make conscious choices about how you live your life—a very big pay-off for a short period of agony.

It has taken a potential disaster to make me realize how not in control we really are. For five years I have waited to have surgery on my eyes. Now it is ten days after the surgery, and I'm still waiting for my vision to improve. My doctor tells me not to worry, but my problem was supposed to have been resolved by now. I just sit and wait, putting everything else on the back burner. This affects all areas of my life, as a husband, father, friend, not to mention employee. I am sorry if I sound hostile, because I am enjoying this class. My life just seems to be on hold as I deal with something that is not under my control.

You don't sound hostile to me. Frightened, disappointed, and hurt, is my projection. And, what you're going through now is exactly why we practice. Someone once said that when you are suffering it is good to remember that it is possible not to suffer, and when you are not suffering it is good to remember that it is possible to suffer. If we wait to take care of our health until we're sick, wait to work on our physical fitness until we're out of shape, wait to attend to our personal relationships until people have left us, life will be very hard. If we remember how fortunate we are when times are good, if we really appreciate the easy, happy, comfortable times, while realizing that this too is impermanent, then we will not be devastated when life brings us the other side of the duality. The Buddha referred to us as children playing in a burning building. Most of us don't wake up until it is too late. But now we have a chance to make a different choice.

I can see that the only thing I can practice controlling are my thoughts. So, that's what I have been practicing all week. I guess what I want is to let the thoughts go so I can just be in awareness.

Instead of trying to control your thoughts, see if you can just notice them. Noticing leaves space for doing other things. You can mow the lawn and notice your thoughts. You can drive the car and notice your thoughts. As you practice, you can listen to someone talk and notice your thoughts. Soon you will be able to talk and still notice your thoughts. As you practice in this way, you will see that thoughts are just thoughts. Thoughts have only the power you give them. If you notice them as they arise and pass away, they can do you no harm. You are not the thoughts, you are the awareness that notices.

THE BUDDHA taught us to live in contemplation of body, feelings, mind, and mind objects. He taught this because all that keeps us in bondage is held (and hidden) in the body, feelings, mind, and mind objects. The way to release ourselves from suffering is to see clearly <u>how</u> this holding is being done, and to cease that holding.

We talk about our conditioned state as "ignorance and delusion" because the whole process of suffering, how we suffer, remains unavailable to us, hidden behind habits and assumptions. We learn to focus our attention on awareness and to be aware of our attention because this is the process for opening up and shedding light on these hidden areas.

Here is what I asked the class to do:

Continue exploring the process of control: How does control exist in your body? In your feelings? In your mind, both as process and content? For example, you worry (process) and there are things (content) that you worry about.

This is not a contest. We watch. We notice. We pay attention to everything so we can see how we are being controlled. We watch so we can see how our attention is used to maintain false assumptions and habits that keep us in familiar, ego-friendly ruts. We're not trying to change, we're learning to SEE.

Responses

The thought of control takes me back to an assumption: I assume a world I control is better than a world I don't. I assume my life would be significantly better if I could control more aspects of it.

I love your awareness that that is an assumption, and I think in our more lucid moments we can be grateful that we are not in control! Life gives us so much more than we would ever think of having for ourselves if our puny little egos were in control of the giving.

Lately, I've realized that my interest in books about positive thinking and affirmation comes from the belief that these things will help me control my life. They promise me that I can have whatever I want as long as I think positively and confidently that it is true. But this idea of positive thinking has become a self-hate racket for me. When bad things happen (things out of my control) I blame myself for not being positive enough.

I find myself projecting this promise of control even when it isn't there. I assume meditation will make me calm, and calmness will lead to greater control, and I'll be more confident at work and in my social life, and everything will be improved all because of meditation! But no one ever claimed that meditation will help my career or my love life. I'm learning to live in a world I can't control, to accept that where I am is where I need to be, and to make the best of what I can.

That is a lot, isn't it? If you continue with nothing other than that (and awareness practice, of course) I suspect you will lead a happy life. You won't be happy because of getting what you want, you will be happy because of the accepting, kind, trusting, open attitude of mind you bring to each day. As I remind people, "It's not what, it's how." Life is a process. If we are accepting and compassionate in our process, the content will become irrelevant. If I love to garden, the plants, the weather, the bugs, the soil, the seasons are not seen as things I must control, they are all part of the process of gardening, which I love.

As for positive thinking and affirmations, it seems to me if we focus on what is so each day, rather than derailing into the self-hating judgment and criticism of conditioning, we'll do just fine. If we walk around all day saying things to ourselves like, "I'll never get a decent job," or, "No one is ever going to want to be with me," that is bound to have an impact on our lives. However, the alternative doesn't need to be an obsessive focus on how ego thinks life has to be for it to be happy. I think the winning alternative is to be in the moment we are in, with our hearts as open as possible, noticing everything, feeling as much gratitude as we can muster for how much goodness there is in life.

The feeling of not having any control is overwhelming sometimes. Today, I got real busy cleaning the house and washing clothes and doing things I know I can "do" so I could feel in control. That is a very old habit: When I feel out of control (never mind that I'm never actually in control, the point is when I FEEL out of control) I start tackling projects, usually cleaning or painting or fixing up things. Then at least my outside doesn't look as chaotic as I feel.

You make a very good point about whether or not one <u>feels</u> in (or out of) control. That is so much of it, isn't it? If things are going pretty much the way I want them to go, I <u>feel</u> in control. The fact that I'm not actually in control isn't a problem because I'm not getting any signals that tell me I'm not in control. No out of control feeling, no problem.

When you mention feeling overwhelmed, I wonder if you experience that as fear. In fact, egocentricity is terrified that you will realize there is nothing wrong with you, no matter how chaotic things look, and then it will lose control of your life.

There is tremendous fear in letting go of control. I hear myself say, "I'll lose my job, everything will pass me by, I'll be perceived as weak. My wife won't love/respect me, I won't get what I want/need, my daughter will grow up wild/undisciplined/ miserable. I will cease to exist." It feels like letting go of control equals death on some level, that there is a need to "hold it all together." Even if holding it together is clearly not working, the alternative seems even more frightening.

Letting go of control equals death for egocentricity, so it is indeed frightening for conditioning. Being tied up in knots over trying to make things go a certain way, then being fearful of the results--when we're caught in that kind of suffering, it's good to remember that soon we will be dead, and we will be dead a long, long time. From that perspective, we are more likely to accept that we have nothing to lose in trying something different. We are miserable now. Could we be more miserable if we tried something else? Maybe, but if so, we can always return to this current, familiar level of misery. However, we might be less miserable or even not miserable at all. What if we let go and all the misery evaporates and we are as happy as all this control was supposed to make us? Remembering how soon and how long we'll be dead can help us be willing to risk letting go now.

I don't know if this falls within the scope of assumptions and control (although it seems like almost everything does!), but I have a problem in this workshop and my spiritual practice in general. As soon as I begin to feel a new level of understanding, it becomes intellectualized, just another thought trophy. There's some part of me who feels he's "got it" as soo as the least intellectual grasp is attained, and then all openness is closed off. At difficult moments, the intellectual understandings of practice feel too dry and fail to provide real connections and paths out of suffering. How can I break past this ego trap?

It's simple: Come back to the breath. Let the one who got the intellectual understanding have it. You had the insight, let him noodle it. You take a long deep breath, look at the moment you're in, remind yourself that this moment is utterly new, that you know nothing because there is nothing to know about what has not yet happened, smile, and get on with your life. It is simple but exceedingly threatening to ego and therefore very challenging to practice.

I have moments of joy when I let go, and I try to remember those moments when I am caught up in controlling behaviors. Sometimes I can let in this different perspective of freedom and joy, and sometimes egocentricity wins out by convincing me that those moments of joy are delusion. I am tearful as I write this. How can I be so mean to myself as to say that joy and freedom are delusions, that it is safer to suffer? This is when compassion arises in me, when I see to what lengths I will go, or egocentricity will go, to be in charge. Why would I do this to myself?

When you say "I," who do you mean? Are you the "I" who is compassionate, accepting, nonjudgmental, unconditional divinity? Are you the "I" who is egocentric, conditioned, desperate to survive at any cost, center of the universe, illusion of a separate self? If you can keep in mind that these two perspectives exist simultaneously (in fact the former contains the latter), you will not have to wonder ever again, "Why would I do this to myself?" From center, all this exists and is just fine.

Hui Neng, one of the great masters of Zen, is famous for saying, "From the beginning no thing is." We make this all up, string it together, and after we have put so much effort into making it into something that is ours, we are very attached to it and believe we must carry it around forever. (A fair description of karma.) As we sit still, we notice that it hangs together only because we continue to project it. If we don't keep the connections together by the force of our will, they fall apart. As they fall apart, as they return to what they essentially are--nothing--all other possibilities are available to us. This is why change, self-improvement, and "efforting" are such a waste of time. All that trying is just another way of holding on to what would go away if we weren't clinging to it.

HANGING IN the dining room of our monastery
is a sign with the sentence, "Love answers all the
questions that judgment fails to hear." When we
look and listen with compassion, we find questions our
judgments fail to recognize, and we sense the
answers to those questions. We can see the fear
and hear the despair behind actions that judgment
would simply write off as selfish or foolish.

In this section, "Pay Attention to Everything," we
have focused so far on the "pay attention" part but
not on the "to everything." Actually, we've been
sneaking up on the "everything" part through
exploring assumptions, habits, and control, but there
is a whole side of those issues that we have not
addressed. What do I not assume? What does my
habit help me avoid? What would be in my life if
control were not an issue?

My teacher used to say, "People die of liking and
disliking." Wanting something to be different from
how it is, believing something could be different
from how it is, is the delusion upon which the illusion
of a separate self is built. Sengtsan, the third
Patriarch of Zen said, "Don't seek after

enlightenment, simply cease to cherish opinions."
Judgment separates; love (compassion) is the
experience of nonseparate reality.

It's now time to bring those three things together:
1. how judgment makes our world small
2. the role of liking and disliking
3. the exploration of that "everything" part of
"pay attention to everything."

A suggestion: Write down the sentence "love answers
all the questions that judgment fails to hear," and
see if that can assist you in expanding your world
view. Ask yourself, if I didn't think I already knew
the answer, what else might be a possibility in this
moment?

Here is what I asked the class to do:

Explore judgment, liking and disliking, and the
"everything" part of pay attention to everything.

1) See if you can notice a judgment, and rather than let the voices start in on you about what a bad person you are for judging, see if you can hold that judgment in place as a line cutting through life, showing you what is on the inside of that line and what is on the outside. See it as a line of demarcation, as a line of separation. For example, if I say to myself, I should be different from the way I am, that judgment creates a line dividing the world/life/me into the ways I am and the ways I should be. All of life will fall on one side or the other of that line. Every person is either the way I/they should be or they are not.

2) Turn your attention to the role of liking and disliking in your life. Bring conscious awareness to what gets a yes and what gets a no from you. I encourage conscious awareness because most liking and disliking goes on just beneath the level of conscious awareness. We see a person, we scan them, judgments are rendered, opinions formed, and they are placed in the plus or minus category without any consciousness on our part. An exercise: Consider for a moment what is your favorite food? Now, consider what is your least favorite food?

Sometime this week would you please eat each of these foods in a slow, mindful, attentive, conscious way and see what it is exactly that makes these particular foods your most and least favorite. Write down your responses.

3) All of this is designed to bring more attention to that everything part of pay attention to everything. So, as you go through the days keep glancing out of the corner of your eye for the things you are conditioned to miss. What sounds don't you hear? What kinds of comments do you ignore? What don't you see? What emotions do you avoid? What do you not allow yourself? What have you closed yourself off to?

Responses

On the liking and disliking, I haven't yet eaten the food that I dislike but I have eaten some that I really like. My thing is this, when I pay attention to the flavors and textures of what I'm eating or whatever I'm doing, I get excited and energized and then quickly overwhelmed and feel like I want this feeling to stop, that it is too much, not sustainable, not real. I have found that with lots of things, if they feel too good, if I get too interested and excited about them, I find myself avoiding them. That sounds like conditioning running my life. It's not okay to be so excited you want to jump up and down, so don't do stuff that makes you feel that way.

Reading this I'm jumping up and down! Yes, yes, yes. Conditioning says," Don't get too excited, don't be too happy, don't do what you love, don't be present, don't pay attention, don't write in responses, YOU'LL BE OUT OF CONTROL!" Well, no, conditioning will no longer be in control.

I remind people who are doing awareness practice that "the container has to expand." As you become more aware, the energy grows. Egocentricity maintains control by getting you to dissipate the extra energy through unconsciousness, feeling bad, self-hate, depression, addictions, etc. That's how it keeps the life force something IT can manage. If you are going to have that extra energy available for yourself, for things like joy and bliss, say, you have to allow the range of acceptable feelings, sensations, and emotions to expand. You have to learn to be ok with feeling great! But it is difficult because feeling good throws conditioning into high gear like nothing else.

I am having some trouble with viewing how I judge things. You see, I am a mental health therapist and we are trained to diagnose, which is to label a set of symptoms. People come into my office and I think "depression" or "marital conflict" or "anxiety." I find it hard to do treatment without naming things. Also, clients who are in pain want answers, they usually are not open to "this is part of the process, just keep going."

Maybe I am missing something here, but observing my assumptions and judgments has caused me to feel like the centipede who was doing fine until someone asked him how he got all of his legs to walk. He started thinking about it and then couldn't do it any more. Now I watch myself driving and wonder at how my arm and feet can work together to shift the car, and find that when I observe (think?) about it, I can hardly do it.

I think this is a wonderful place to be! If the centipede had stayed with awareness practice he would have discovered that his problem was thinking he needed to step outside life, create a subject/object relationship with his legs, and go up into his conditioning to know how to do something that is not a problem if egocentricity is not involved. When he saw that process for what it was, he would have dropped the whole thing and walked off just fine. The real point of that story is that in his self-consciousness he became like a human! He stopped being authentically in the moment he was in and turned to what he <u>should</u> know in order to act. Before we bring conscious, compassionate awareness to ourselves, we are not natural at all! Quite the opposite. We are programmed, unconscious, robotic, and self-absorbed.

At the risk of causing offense, I don't offer "answers" to people who are in pain, and I find that people are very open to hearing that where they are is "part of the process." I don't believe that there is anything wrong with people. I find that people are comforted by being with someone who knows there's nothing wrong with them. They are in pain, maybe confused, unsure, anxious, depressed, whatever, but there isn't anything WRONG with them. They may benefit from some assistance in sorting out where they are and where they want to be, but they feel encouraged by a person who knows they can see for themselves, and that they are perfectly adequate to their lives.

Buddhism has long, and often, been called the first therapy and the Buddha the first therapist. So, I don't hold a belief that labels are anything but limits, and as such I find them annoyingly unhelpful. I hope you will keep experimenting and let me know what you find. We regularly have folks in meditation who have had the experience of ego deciding that it's going to take over the practice of breathing. We can always recognize them, they're the ones coughing and choking!

I am surprised again and again by how much judgment I am ready to apply to what I do, feel, think, want. And I am resonating with your question, who is this person who feels judged and who is this person who thinks she can do the judging?

Stepping back as you have described opens up life in a way that is inexpressible, for me anyway! We spend our conditioned lives believing this, wanting that, fearing them, clinging to those, avoiding the rest, and then we take that half-step back and, miracle of miracles, wonder "What's going on here? Why do I do that? Where did I learn that? What makes me think that? How do I know any of this is true? Why am I willing to kill myself over a bunch of ideas that may be false?????" Ah, sweet dawning of expanding awareness. Ah, the gratitude for that larger perspective.

I ate a beet two days ago as one of my least favorite foods. A memory arose of not liking beets as a child and having to eat them anyway. In my mind a little girl said, "Don't hit me. Don't kill me," and my shoulder tensed. So, perhaps one of the things that my habits help me avoid is re-experiencing the pain of childhood, as though something is trying to protect me from that. On the other hand, I'd rather face that experience and feel that pain, than live in unconscious fear of that pain and have a limited life. I learned that no one hit me and I didn't die from eating beets. They're just beets.

That kind of experience can be the beginning, or the continuation, of conditioning. Something happens and we tense up in an effort to keep that same thing from happening again. You've probably noticed that doesn't work. The same thing never happens again, so our preparation is for naught, and new things come in that we didn't expect, constantly surprising us. In theory all this tensing and protecting is designed to take care of the traumatized child, but it actually KEEPS the child in a state of trauma. But you have seen that when you "go back" and get that little girl who cringes against being hit or killed because she displeased an authority, and you reassure her, comfort her, and stay with her until she trusts that you won't abandon her, both of you are liberated. If she remains hidden behind that "habit," both of you remain in bondage.

When I step back and look at the **process** of like and dislike, and not just the **content**, it creates enough space to not take the content so seriously. I don't have any illusion that I will always prefer eating chocolate eclairs to raw carrots, but when it has to ALWAYS be eclairs instead of carrots it becomes a problem.

Right you are. And, it is good to remain open. Some day you might actually PREFER the carrots. It could happen. It happened to me.

I finally took a bite of my least favorite food, coleslaw, and explained to my friend that this class was asking us to look at our assumptions. Funny that I hated coleslaw all of these years because it really wasn't that bad. She asked me what I didn't like about it, and I explained that I heard it was made by being put into wooden barrels and sitting so that the bacteria could break down the cabbage. (I myself thought this odd because I eat yogurt BECAUSE it has bacteria in it.) She interrupted me, "That's not coleslaw! You are talking about sauerkraut!" We both laughed. Even though this is a silly example, think of the years of my life wasted that I could have been having delicious coleslaw experiences! Those tricky assumptions. And yes, I'll work up the nerve to eat some sauerkraut.

Ah, the sky's the limit!

THE CIRCLE of Acceptance is an exercise I
have worked with for several years. As with many
other things, "accepting" or "rejecting" are largely
unconscious, conditioned reactions to circumstance
instead of present moment choice. When we view
with compassionate awareness what we accept and
what we reject, we have the opportunity to let go
of our resistance and judgment of people, things,
and situations we might have been struggling with all
our lives.

Here is what I asked the class to do:

Get pencil and paper and draw a circle six or eight
inches in diameter. This is the "circle of
acceptance." Write down inside the circle everything
that is currently inside your circle of acceptance.
Write down outside the circle everything that is
currently outside your circle of acceptance. Take as
long as you need, and when you are through, put the
paper aside.

Sit quietly and turn your attention to your breath. Take ten long, full breaths before you proceed any further, letting go of everything except focusing on your breathing.

Now, look back through your life and bring into conscious awareness some of the challenges and struggles you have faced. See if you can remember the sequence of events and how you felt about what was going on. Perhaps there are particular sensory memories that go with these situations, or perhaps there is humor or sadness or a particular emotion. As you look, consider how you have grown and changed as a result of having these experiences.

Take three or four deep breaths, and, letting all that go, pick up your paper and pencil and see if there are things outside your circle of acceptance that you would now be willing to place inside. Considering that "love answers all the questions that judgment fails to hear," is there anything else you would be willing to bring inside the circle of acceptance? Are there things you are willing to extend compassion to? Remember, putting something inside the circle doesn't mean you have to like or condone it; it just means you accept that this, too, is.

Responses

There is nothing outside my circle that I would ever want inside of it. Violence, intolerance, rudeness, homophobia, greed and materialism are what I wrote outside the circle. Inside I wrote: trust, honesty, diversity, compassion, kindness, ability, communication, understanding, solitude.

Who is that "I" who makes that distinction? What happens to "you" when you are one of those unacceptable ways?

The hardest thing to accept is myself. I have so many judgments about what I should be doing, how I look, etc. How can I accept people around me with love and compassion, but not myself? Am I fooling myself with this talk, cause if I don't love me, how do I know enough to love them? And if I judge myself so harshly, how can I say I don't judge them? This current of dissatisfaction with self has screamed at me all my life, and I know it's that ego part that wants to stay in control. I just want to hug myself and tell me that it's all going to be okay, and when I meditate that's what happens. Where do I go with this?

I think you've answered your own questions pretty clearly. Where do you go with this? You go to the mind of meditation ALL THE TIME. If you have a parent whom you love and are committed to who is a bigot, can you let that parent say outrageous, ignorant, hateful things and not be confused that that ignorance makes them unlovable or someone you have to constantly correct? Can you just let what they say roll off your back, knowing that you are here to do your own work, not theirs? If so, apply that to egocentricity. When it says vicious, ugly, cruel things about you, ignore it. "That's just ego, that has nothing to do with me." And refer to it as "ego" rather than "I." "Ego has so many judgments about what I should be doing, how I look. Ego can accept people around me with love and compassion, but not me. If ego judges me so harshly, can I say ego doesn't judge them?" The "I" of ego and the "me" who is trashed are, experientially, different. Does this lead to an illusion of separation? No, believing "you" are that voice of ego actually perpetuates the belief in separation. Hug that "myself," meditate together, and don't stop.

After moving to a different part of the country, where the standard of living, educational level, and social norms are close to that of Third World countries, I witnessed what I consider to be severe child abuse of more than one child. The children are not mine, or even blood relatives, but I am not able to shake off judgments I have or let go of wanting to control things.

At first I took the stance of a witness, with no need or desire to change the system. I was able to let go of thoughts as they came in and find compassion for the people. When it felt appropriate and I was asked, I did whatever I could for whomever.

In the last month I feel unable to keep the focus on myself for all the pain I feel having seen so much unnecessary violence, especially within families. I sit and I sit, and I let the feelings move through me and try and let them go. And when there is not pain there is such anger that it almost paralyses me.

Besides my breathing, I have been trying to focus on nature, a single bloom or blade of grass, or the mighty oak trees in the front yard, or the tremendous beauty I see in my wife. Even then I am not immune from the rest of it creeping in. I keep letting go and going back to my breathing or a flower, pausing only long enough to sit for a moment and be aware of my feelings of total despair.

I cannot for the life of me distinguish between a small circle cut up into parts and the great circle of life I am moment by moment moving through. I can find no dividing line.

I would suggest that you have found the dividing line --this is ok, that is not. That which I consider beautiful is acceptable, that which I see as violent is not. If I did not have to witness all this violence in other people, I would not have to feel these feelings inside me. "I feel unable to focus on myself for having seen so much unnecessary violence." Where does "myself" end? Is not this pain, this violence, inside me? Who knows what is "necessary" and what is "unnecessary"? It is hard, very hard, to be grateful for life circumstances that put us in touch with paralyzing anger or total despair, but those circumstances are essential if we truly want to end suffering.

In our privileged First World neighborhoods, so many of us have the ability to insulate ourselves from the level of suffering, greed, hate, and delusion that much of the world knows to be day-to-day life. I have lived in California all my life and I can promise you there are "Third World countries" just across every freeway, on the other side of every town. It's just that we can look the other way and our suffering, our greed, hate, and delusion is "white collar," done with stocks, credit cards, and checkbooks. The beatings we give and get don't leave visible scars. Our hatred takes the form of omission rather than commission. We can look so fine! Then we get a chance to check out our assumptions, and it can be hard to say thank you. I admire your courage in continuing to look.

By eating foods that I like and dislike, I found that the likes and dislikes keep me from being aware. Making judgments did constrict my world, but in drawing the circle of acceptance, I resisted some ideas ever being included in the circle. When you asked, "What will you do when you find these things in yourself?" I realized that I frequently put myself outside the circle, as shown by my inability to forgive myself for any violation of my principles.

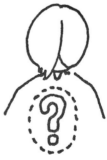

Once again, the burning question is "Who is this I?" Do you know what I mean by that? Who is an I who could put a myself outside anything? If these are two folks, which it sure sounds as if they are, who put one in charge of the other? Why does one get to judge and one have to be judged? Who is the I who won't forgive me?

If a group of people came into town and took it over, decided who was good and who was bad, who was innocent and who was guilty, who gets praise and who gets blame, who is rewarded and who is punished, wouldn't you want to know who they are and where they get off? C'mon, at least ask for some identification!

I reached an insight today. Here it is: I'm willing to do almost anything for this class. I'll ponder assumptions, control, habits. I'll draw an acceptance circle and put obnoxious things in there. I'll bear my soul. I'll munch and meditate on onion rings, a favorite food. But I'm damned if I'll eat Brussels sprouts! Having come to this insight, I started laughing. Is one of the keys to relief of suffering perhaps not to take ourselves too seriously?

Oh, indeed. Only ego takes itself seriously. I often kid people in group discussions that when they are very "identified" with egocentricity, above all else, they must not laugh! The only way we can stay identified with conditioning is to be very seriously focused on how serious the issue is. When we step back and see how silly we are, how ridiculous that little ego is, strutting around there at the center of the universe, we laugh, and suffering falls away.

I probably do not accept myself because I can never live up to the standards that ego sets for me. Ego wants me to control the world and won't be happy until I die trying! (I hope I'm exaggerating a little.) I'm not sure how to bring myself into my own circle of acceptance, along with many other people that I have judged harshly. I feel great anxiety writing all of this. I can only imagine what my life would be if I were free of this need of approval from "out there."

I suspect you are "imagining" that life from a very real place. It might be interesting to put your circle of acceptance where you can see it often, and put "people who don't approve of me" in big letters <u>inside</u> the circle. Then just watch what happens. If it is true that "love answers all the questions that judgment fails to hear," I'll bet you will be getting some clarity on this issue soon.

The Second Key

Believe
nothing

WE "BELIEVE" as a way of not facing the very uncomfortable (to egocentricity) fact that we don't know. Life never repeats itself. Each split second everything in the universe is different. Each moment is brand new; it could be anything. Not having a guarantee about what is coming next, we imagine what will happen (we project the past into the future) and cling to a belief that our imaginings are true. Then believing is supposed to make us feel more secure, but if we believe something we don't know to be true, and may suspect is not true, anxiety, not security, is the result.

As a culture we operate out of the assumption that if enough people believe something it must be true. The process of group assuming and believing seems to work, because when people believe something is true, they *experience* whatever it is as true. For instance, if I told a group of people that the individual I was bringing to speak with them is one of the wisest, clearest, most awakened masters living today, they would hear what that individual said as wise, assuming they believed my judgment. On the other hand, if I informed the group that the person I was bringing to speak with them is a primary example of extreme intelligence masking delusion, they would hear everything that was said through the filter of "this person is deluded."

The "truth" and "knowing" are so important to us because they perpetuate the belief that it is possible to control life. If I know enough, I can be safe. If I have enough accurate information, I can do the right thing and get the result I want.

HERE ARE A FEW of the ways we attempt to control the outcome of the next moments in order to make life fit with our beliefs: selective perception, tensed muscles, self-hate, superstition, and self-control. "If I make myself (and those around me) be the way I 'should' be, then my life will be the way I believe it should be and I will get what I want." In this way we manage to avoid seeing what is so and are able to continue to choose our beliefs over our experience. "When life doesn't go the way it should, it's my fault. If I were better, smarter, stronger (whatever), this wouldn't be happening. If things aren't the way they should be, it's proof that there's something wrong with me."

This is a child's view of life. It seems secure; it perpetuates suffering.

Here is what I asked the class to do:

Make a list of the things you know to be true. Pay attention to how you do this.

Responses

Things I know to be true:
I was born
I will die
I am human
I am alive
I want to be happy
I want all other humans to be happy also. (Fair is fair. Besides, if they are happy they are less likely to pick on me.)

There are those who might point us in the direction of realizing that there is no "I" to be born and thus no "I" to die. What is a human? What does it mean to be human? If we are talking about labels, then we know the "name" for everything, except that things are only named these names in English. In other languages they are named something else, except in cultures where those things don't exist. "I" is this "thing" that is called "human." What does that mean? If "I" is an illusion, where does that leave us humans? Apparently the genes of a chimpanzee are more than 99% identical to ours. Still, they're not "human," so instead of "life, liberty, and the pursuit of happiness," they get the destruction of their species in laboratories. As recently as the 1930s people were arguing whether or not people of African descent were fully human. The Greeks debated whether women were. I don't mean to be hard on you. I just want us to consider what we're saying, thinking, and believing.

"I want to be happy" is one of my personal favorites. We all say we want to be happy; people would stop talking to us if we said, "Well, no, actually, I would rather be locked into the suffering of my egocentric, karmic conditioning, but I have to say I want to be happy because that's the socially acceptable thing to do." But we proceed to do everything possible to avoid happiness. Happiness is really easy. All we have to do is accept everything exactly as it is--but this is very unpopular as a life choice. In seventeenth century Japan, there was a Zen Master named Bankei. When he died a blind beggar who lived near the steps of the temple where Bankei taught said of the Master, "When something good happened to someone I only heard happiness in his voice, and when something bad happened, I only heard sadness." This has been passed down through the years because it is such a remarkable statement about a person. We live in a me-first, not-enough-to-go-around, fiercely competitive, greed-hate-and-delusion-rule world. Do we really want people to be happy? All people? Even the ones who aren't doing it right? Even the ones who don't deserve to be happy?

I live as though everything egocentricity tells me is true.

Sounds like you're on to it. My encouragement: Write it all down. Make big charts and hang them on the wall. Make big lists of: Things I Believe, Things I Don't Believe but Listen to Anyway, and Really Stupid Things That Go Through My Mind That Conditioning Would Like Me to Believe. If you are a dedicated kind of person, you can go back through periodically and revise the lists. Just to stay current!

My list is short:
I love my wife and children
This moment is all there is.

I am sure that that is your experience and I would not disagree for the world, so I will talk about me and the part of me who might make those statements.

I love my family. And because I know that, believe that, assume that, I don't need to spend much time or energy exploring what that actually MEANS to me and whether or not my life is in keeping with that meaning. I can do what I do and say what I say without scrutiny, because I KNOW I love my family. What I need to do in this situation may not make them happy, but if it feels un-loving to them, well, they're wrong, because I know that I love them. I may not always be considerate, or sensitive, or available, but that's not a problem, because I DO love them. In other words, without a great deal of observation, my love can give me (more accurately, my conditioning) permission to go unconscious and do whatever, because whatever I do happens in a context of love [as I (who?) define it].

An amazing practice in a relationship is to sit down with a loved one and ask, What makes you feel loved? What do I DO that makes you feel loved. What do I do that makes you feel unloved? What habits would you like me to change? What assumptions would you like me to drop? How do you need to be listened to? In this way I can begin to see if I am loving me or loving my loved one.

This moment is all there is. Do I know that? Do I believe that? How well could I know that if my life doesn't reflect that knowing? How much do I believe that if my life is not lived according to my belief? I know this moment is all there is, I believe this moment is all there is, and I live as if this moment doesn't matter at all.

My relationship between what I believe and what I know became a bit clearer as I sat in meditation today. I know that I am not fat; I believe that I am way overweight and it means I'll be abandoned and lost forever. I know that I'm very okay alone; I believe that I have to see and be seen in order to survive. I know that I won't go insane; I (truly) believe that my thoughts will overtake me and lead me down the path of obsessive and compulsive living. I know that I have TMJ and that from time to time it flares up. I really believe that one of these times the jaw will break down on me and I'll never be able to chew, talk, or live normally.

For me to know things does not have the same power or strength as the beliefs. I can sit and pay attention and get calm for a bit, but when the beliefs instill panic in me, the knowing does not help.

I hold on to one knowing that I read in one of your books: Believing in God is different from knowing God. That is more powerful for me each time I think of it. I wonder if it can be true that the knowing of me, the physical me, will be powerful enough to have these beliefs fade.

If you stay with this work, yes, the "knowing" of you, the body/mind "you" of the present will be (is) powerful enough to cause you to lose interest in beliefs.

It is so hard to imagine while we're trapped in the grip of egocentric conditioning that one day we will prefer a world in which none of that exists. I suggest that to folks and often get a response of, "But where's the passion in life?" I can assure you that the choices are not to be either caught in the torture of karmic conditioning or dropped into a void of tapioca pudding. The present is vibrant, alive, thrilling, exquisite, subtle, and compelling. Compared to that, the "excitements" of the world of egocentricity are tedious. Soon, egocentricity will pull out all the stops and you simply won't be interested.

It remains so interesting to me: Why do we need "truth"? How can we say this is true and that is not? Aren't we just attempting to continue the world of duality? If we were to use a word such as God for All That Is, can we say, this is God and that is not? This is All That Is, but that is not All That Is. How can that be? All That Is, by definition has no "other." Yet, that's frightening, isn't it? What happens to us if everything really is ONE? If this is a circle with no remainder, what happens to all that is outside the circle?

OFTEN, PEOPLE ask me how I know what to do, how I make decisions. "How can you tell when what you are doing is coming from center?" folks ask. Their faces fall when I tell that that I don't know, can't know, and don't even want to know. "Well, how can you tell if you should do one thing or another?" We hit frustration when I reiterate that I can't tell. (I suspect that this the point at which some people head off in pursuit of a better spiritual teacher!) However, it remains my experience that I can be as still, present, and disidentified as I can be, something occurs to me in the moment, and I move in that direction. If someone pins me down about why I am doing what I am doing, my response is often something along the lines of, "Well, it just feels like the direction to go." Doesn't sound very decisive, but here's what I've noticed over the years: When I am convinced that I am coming from a clear, centered place, and that this is, for sure, the right thing to do, I am lost in a world of greed, hate, and delusion. The more right I think I am, the more wrong I turn out to be. When I'm in that, "Well, I don't know, it seems like the thing to do" mode, I can be pretty sure everything is going to be just fine.

Is that a form of knowing? Yes. The difference is, there's no "one" to know. Egocentricity is right and sure and positive; the moment is fluid and without investment.

Here is what I asked the class to do:

1. Pick one thing you know to be true. Choose something small.
2. How do you know this is true?
3. Go through the steps (the process) you take to determine this is true.

For you, what is the difference between knowing something is true and believing it is true?

Responses

In investigating my assumptions, I find I cannot know that any of them, or anything I "believe," is really true. My husband wants to circumcise our unborn son, who is due any day now. I have wrestled with this issue almost since the pregnancy began. I have let go of every assumption and belief I have around this issue, even the very hardest for me: that my role is to protect my child from pain. When I let go and accept the "truth" (?) that I don't know what my child will experience if he is circumcised, that I am projecting my own pain onto him, I do experience freedom and openness. But either my heart or my conditioning (which?) soon tells me this just isn't so, that it's denial, and I am frightened not to adhere to this voice that says, "It's painful, don't do it."

This goes right to the heart of it, doesn't it? At the Monastery we call this experience the "really, really, really, true" experience, meaning that it just seems so believable, how can it NOT be "true"? It is one of the toughest places in practice. Fortunately we have some clues that can help us as we attempt to sit still and discern what is of conditioning and what is of the heart.

The first clue is that the heart never argues. The heart never accuses ("that isn't so, it's denial"). The second clue is that we are not afraid of the heart, probably because it never threatens. The third clue is the order of events: You feel a freedom and openness and then the voices come in to talk you out of your experience.

Please hear that I am not speaking at all to the content of the issue. One of the things that, to me, makes this so painful is that you and your husband are on opposites sides of the issue. I don't know if this will be helpful, but here is something I encourage couples to consider as they look at an issue such as this. Ordinarily when we are in disagreement over an issue, we accomplish this by putting the issue between us, getting on opposite sides of the issue, and arguing over it. It can be helpful to put the issue out in front of you, sit close together, and solve the issue together as a team, from the same side. That can be easier than it seems because you are on the same side, you both want the best for your son and for each other. You each hold a different view of what that best is. It could be fun (as a person who adores awareness, I admittedly have an odd view of fun) to write out all of the reasons each of you has for your perspective, then give one another your list, and spend ten or fifteen minutes arguing for the other's viewpoint. All of these activities expand awareness, reveal conditioned beliefs, and flush out egocentricity.

Here is my own personal take on the situation you're in: Your child will benefit enormously throughout his life from having parents who will bring conscious, compassionate awareness to even the most difficult of times, and would suffer greatly if he were raised by people whose principles were of higher value to them than extending lovingkindness to others. If he sees modeled for him people who will deeply question their own assumptions, let go of the most closely held beliefs, go into frightening, threatening territory in order to be as loving as they can be, that is one lucky child. But if he sees people who make decisions based on fear, he will grow up to do the same.

The truth, as I see it, is that we do not know and we must accept with as open a heart as we can, whatever is, regardless. If I am to assist in the ending of suffering, I must let go of all I cling to that is suffering, regardless of how right I am, or how wrong someone else is, or even how I might be judged by others. I get so upset when people abuse children or animals or minorities or the environment that I hate those people and wish them dead. Many would think of that response as noble, certainly understandable, the kind of reaction we need for things to change. But we know that is not so. Hate is hate, it doesn't matter what the object is. Showing disregard for those who show disregard advances nothing. How is the world a better place if I become cruel in response to my suffering over the cruelty of others?

There's an old Zen story that speaks to this:

Zenkai, the son of a samurai, journeyed to Edo and there became the retainer of a high official. He fell in love with the official's wife and was discovered. In self-defense, he slew the official. Then he ran away with the wife.

Both of them later became thieves. But the woman was so greedy that Zenkai grew disgusted. Finally, leaving her, he journeyed far away to the province of Buzen, where he became a wandering mendicant.

To atone for his past, Zenkai resolved to accomplish some good deed in his lifetime. Knowing of a dangerous road over a cliff that
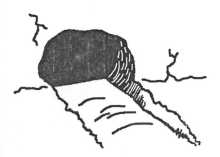 had caused the death and injury of many persons, he resolved to cut a tunnel through the mountain there.

Begging food in the daytime, Zenkai worked at night digging his tunnel. When thirty years had gone by, the tunnel was 2,280 feet long, 20 feet high, and 30 feet wide.

Two years before the work was completed, the son of the official he had slain, who was a skillful swordsman, found Zenkai out and came to kill him in revenge.

"I will give you my life willingly," said Zenkai, "only let me finish this work. On the day it is completed, you may kill me."

So the son awaited the day. Several months passed and Zenkai kept on digging. The son grew tired of doing nothing and began to help with the digging. After he had helped for more than a year, he came to admire Zenkai's strong will and character.

At last the tunnel was completed and the people could use it and travel in safety.

"Now cut off my head," said Zenkai, "my work is done."

"How can I cut off my own teacher's head?" asked the young man with tears in his eyes.

So what's the right thing to do? Who's right? Who's wrong? As a friend of mine says, "You never know the end of the story."

This morning as I drove my son to school I said to him "I wish you would. . . " when I suddenly saw that I was about to rehash a belief. I stopped and told him, "I guess it doesn't matter what I wish". Not only did we have a nicer ride together, but also I started to question the whole content of what I was going to say. Do I really want to impose my perfectionist conditioning on him? Am I really doing the same behavior I find objectionable in him? All that insight just from catching a "belief" about to spew.

This awareness practice is practical, isn't it? What a bind parents are in. We feel terrible about all the rotten stuff we are passing along to our kids (we had parents so we know what we're doing to our kids), and at the same time conditioning uses every trick in the book to keep us from knowing what's going on with us. How can I know what my conditioning is doing to my kids if I don't know what my conditioning is doing to me? That's why I encourage parents to consider that not only will we pass along our conditioning. (I have a therapist friend who says, "The given is you will screw up your kids. Do it in the way that is most comfortable for you.") but we can also pass along to them a model of adults who continue to grow in awareness, take responsibility, and let go in an effort to be the best people they can be.

What came to my mind upon reading the assignment was how often I say "I can't believe. . ." (that this is happening, that I did that, etc.). How is it that no matter how often someone does the same thing, I still "can't believe it"? Why can't I detach from other people's behaviors and either not respond at all or say, "Oh, there she is, just being herself"?

I, too, have noticed that response and marveled at it. What an interesting view of the world it maintains. It has occurred to me that if we would stop being shocked by violence, hatred, cruelty, and greed, we might acknowledge those tendencies in us as people and take steps to see what makes us this way. Instead, day after day, year after year, we read or hear headlines announcing the latest horrific act as if it is a surprise. "Oh, my god, someone killed all those people." "Oh, no, someone committed a heinous crime." "Oh, my, someone was hugely dishonest!" We are shocked and appalled and amazed by how THEY can be.

I guess I just don't know "what I know to be true" about death or the possible consequences of not playing by ego's rules. (I just saw the assumption that one has anything to do with the other!) That's the threat, isn't it? Ego says, "You play by my rules or you'll get exterminated." Maybe death is just death and there's nothing else attached to it.

And if that is so, that death is just death, can life be just life? Can you then just live, knowing some day you will die and when that happens, that happens? Here's the deal: If you stop playing by ego's rules, ego will die. So, it is giving you very accurate information when it lets you know, "Play by the rules, or die." Someone will die; it just won't be you. In fact, when ego ceases to be in charge of your life, you will be alive for the first time.

I know I breathe. I know because when I put my attention on the breath, I'm breathing. What about when I'm not paying attention to the breath? I know I breathe then because I'd die if I didn't. But that's an assumption, based on what I've been taught about human anatomy. How do I know that at least sometimes I'm only imagining that I breathe? This gets creepy.

Ah, that's one of those odd conclusions, isn't it? Lao Tse talked about not knowing if he is a man dreaming he is a butterfly or a butterfly dreaming it is a man. Is that creepy or fascinating? If we are butterflies dreaming we are people, couldn't we start having a lot more fun?

I know I like to be out working in the garden in the morning. How do I know? I will sometimes go out there before work even if I haven't really made the time for it. It feels good to be outside. A feeling of peace stays with me for a while afterward.

Who is the "I" who likes to be in the garden? Someone who is quiet, solitary, enjoys watching growth (even weeds). When I am there in the garden, moving from task to task, it seems like being aware and centered, but I am not sure. The feeling of peace in the garden is not different from the feeling of peace that comes when I am paying attention to the kids, just being with them, the feeling when I am absorbed in what I am doing at work--but that morning sunshine is so nice. . .

 How about this? I experience these movements, these tasks, the children, the garden, the sunshine, and those experiences are the same as what is called "I." Working in the garden/pleasure/morning sunshine equals "me." Is there anything in that to "know"? Or does the

knowing happen when there is a "me" separate from garden/pleasure/morning sunshine?

In reading over some of the class responses to what they believe to be true and your responses to the responses, I found myself getting a little peeved. I thought, "For Pete's sake, we have to believe some things are true." Like believing that when I step out of bed there will be a floor for me to step on. Or that when I put one foot in front of another the earth will support me. Or if I am headed to my bank that the bank will be there.

I just sat with my peevishness for a while. I realized that my assumption was that if I didn't believe these things to be true, I would be paralyzed with fear. Then I sat with that assumption for a while. The bank I'm heading for could have burned down during the night. There could be an earthquake and the ground beneath me would not support my step. I could be driving down the street and have a sinkhole open up in front of me and be sucked down into the earth. I don't know!

It comes back to being in the present, doesn't it? I can believe or not believe that the ground will support me. It really doesn't matter what I believe, because it either will or it won't. What I can do is say I will put one foot in front of the other and be present with what happens. I don't mean thinking about it, like, "Okay, now I am going to put my foot down on the earth. Will it support me? Now I am stepping out of bed, will the floor be there?" That would make me crazy. I mean allowing myself to believe these things and yet not believe at the same time.

I love the idea of the drive to the bank becoming an adventure. Will it be there, or won't it? Not worrying about it, kind of making a game out of it.

This is what I love about your process: Something arises (from the class, from within yourself, or from wherever), you have a conditioned reaction, and you keep watching and questioning. "How do I know that? Do I know that? Why do I believe that? What if that isn't true?"

An attitude of not knowing is just realistic. We don't know. I think the thing that makes us so anxious and insecure is that rather than face not knowing, we believe something we know is not true. What we believe may have been so in one moment, but then we drag that belief around through moments in which it is not true. Again, believing is supposed to make us more secure, but if you're believing something you know deep down is not true, anxiety, not security, is the result. Little kids tend not to be anxious until they get information that there is something to worry about. All creatures have a built-in survival response that enables us to be alert to danger--conditioning turns that into fear that controls our lives even when nothing is going on. It is true that anything could happen in any moment, but that makes life an exciting adventure, not a fearful thing from which we need to cringe and try to hide.

Well, I think I finally found something that I feel comfortable saying I know to be true: I know the love my dog has for me.

I would say that the love of your dog is a projection, but that the fact that it's a projection doesn't mean it isn't true. We know that someone is loving someone! I am still curious to know how it aids your life to turn that into a belief. The dog loves you. You see that. Why is it necessary to believe?

In reaching for something absolute, I came up with laws of nature. If I drop an object it will fall; velocity and mass affect momentum, etc. Then I realized that's so only on this planet at this time. So, basically the only absolute "know" I could think of was if I sit down on this stone step right now it will hold me up. But when I question who is the "I" sitting on the step. . . well? Maybe I can't even say that. I think this is kinda cool.

I agree wholeheartedly. Being present, paying attention to everything, believing nothing that separates us from anything, is infinitely cooler than shrinking into the nightmare of ignorance and delusion. We have nothing to fear. We have no reason not to move full-tilt into each miraculous, amazing, wondrous moment of life.

Let's say I am out hiking and I come to the edge of a cliff. My belief is that if I step off that cliff I am going to fall. Now, angels may come down to swoop me up, I could grab onto a branch, and on and on, but as I see it, I AM going to fall. In that moment, how is not believing going to serve me? The same thing with walking out into traffic or driving out onto the tracks of a moving train. I can't say with absolute certainty what will happen, but I CAN have a pretty good idea what is going to happen. How do we deal with the physical realities? To say that if we drop a rock from a window that it may or may not fall, what if we drop that rock on that basis and it lands on someone's head and injures or kills them? How are we then not responsible for that? I don't feel that a defense would be that "nothing is true." I'm trying to sort out all of this and would like some guidance.

Your question is perfect. Here is the answer. Egocentricity, karmic conditioning, the illusion of being separate from life wants to claim that we need to rely on what it "knows," on its ability to figure out, control, and predict, RATHER THAN THE INHERENT INTELLIGENCE THAT IS YOUR AUTHENTIC NATURE.

WHY DO YOU NEED TO DRAG AROUND A BELIEF SYSTEM TO KEEP YOU FROM STEPPING OFF A CLIFF?

You won't step off that cliff because you are an intelligent, aware, present being. If you do step off that cliff it is because egocentric, karmic conditioning has you off wool-gathering about something in the past or future and has you so caught up, mesmerized, and thoroughly bamboozled, you don't notice the cliff you're stepping off of!!!!!!

Egocentricity wants you to believe that the beliefs that it holds in place, through fear, are keeping you safe. Since fear IS egocentricity, that puts egocentricity right at the center of everyone's life.

You know what you know from your experience. Your experience is your experience. It may not even be true (as in the only possibility from that moment), but it is your experience. There is no reason to put it in stone. There is no reason to believe it. It is good to be open to the possibility that that might be true again. It is good to be open to the possibility that that might not be true again.

I AM FOND of encouraging people to consider that if they never had another thought in their lives, they would be more intelligent than they can possibly imagine.

How can that be so? Because intelligence is present moment clarity, which IS greater than the sum total of all that has come before, all that is now, and all that ever could be.

If you consider "heroes" (in my case they are spiritual, but heroes exist in every walk of life), the thing they have in common is warrior fearlessness. By fearless I mean that if they felt terror, the feeling would only serve to spur them on. They go where others will not. They do what others believe they cannot. They are not stopped by what others believe, by what others have tried to get them to believe, or even by their own beliefs (in the form of limitations). They trust. They are open. And, I would bet they share this in common: However they might talk about it, they live to be in the present. Safety, security, knowing, and being right are synonyms for death.

Here is what I asked the class to do:

Today you live each moment. You know nothing, so there is nothing to keep straight in your head. Since there's nothing you should know, there is no possibility that you should have known better. You believe nothing, so everything is possible. You're not holding onto anything, so you're available for the "anything" that CAN happen.

You are present, open, and spontaneous, able to go with any twist or turn of life. Your mind is fresh and supremely creative because it is not limited by any preconceptions.

You are not worried, anxious, or afraid since you hold no beliefs that there are situations you won't be able to handle, and your EXPERIENCE is that you have always been equal to life. You are at ease and comfortable because that is the natural state of your body, emotions, and mind, and you have no reason to be otherwise.

Responses

A belief that I am completely able to handle any situation that happens without thought is so foreign to me that when I repeat it to myself I have a reaction similar to making the statement "I now have the ability to transform my body into any shape I desire!" A big "Yeah, sure" follows. I don't yet believe this statement.

One of my favorite stories is of Jesus sending out the disciples to preach his message. It was a dangerous time and they were justifiably afraid. They wanted to know what should they say if they were caught and put in jail. Jesus encouraged them to take no thought of what they would say because when the time came what they needed would be given to them. This is an extraordinary message for all of us because it is as true today as it was then and it is as true for Buddhists as for Christians. The moment provides. If we come into the moment with nothing, everything we need will be there for us. If we come in with what we think is a better idea about what the moment will require, the moment acquiesces, and we get to have what we thought would be best. It never is.

But we must prove that to ourselves. There is no way around it. If the likelihood of this theory speaks to your innate intelligence, you will approach this with what some folks call faith, and the whole thing will be easier for you. Without that faith, I can't imagine anyone being willing to try it, but maybe they would. There you are standing in front of whomever, without a thought in your head, waiting for whatever the moment provides. In the beginning that can be a long agonizing time. After a while it becomes supremely restful.

Approaching meditation with awareness was like I had never meditated before, because I was curious to see what meditation is like. I saw that I have all these preconceived notions about it. I have been trying too hard to meditate, which of course creates an "I" meditating. It felt very liberating just to sit there and just watch everything that is going on. I saw ego talking and trying to think, and I would just watch it. It would actually say, "You are getting sleepy, you are getting sleepy"—trying to hypnotize me and take me out of the moment. And ego would comment on everything I saw.

Excellent. You are taking meditation out of ego's list of "things to do" and dropping the standards that only conditioning would be holding. Takes the whole thing to a new level.

Maybe I don't understand what you mean by staying in the moment. To me it sounded as though we were supposed to only pay attention to this moment. I can't get through the day without doing some planning and anticipating of the next moment. What am I missing here? (Probably a lot!)

You are believing things you don't know. You think you know what you believe. You don't have your own experience, and so you have only what you've been told is so. Try it. As the commercials used to say, you'll like it.

I have often wondered if other people saw and experienced a mountain or a table, for example,` the way I did, or did they have an entirely different way of seeing/experiencing and we describe them in such a way that we think we have a common experience. I have also wondered what is the effect/impact on the mountain or the table, based on our collective way of seeing/experiencing them. Of course, I don't really know what is true, but I think that my experience of what is real is constantly changing.

"Truth" has no application. Truth is process, not content. Truth is the process of clarity, of expansiveness, of unity without separation. WHAT is seen in a moment of seeing is irrelevant--the SEEING is all. It is for that reason that there is no application.

In a moment of blinding insight you SEE. You KNOW. But there is no one to know and nothing to know. There is no knowledge. Nothing of the content of the seeing can (truthfully) leave the moment because it is irrelevant. Anything could have been the content for that process. In a moment of clarity you could read a cereal box and realize the truth of everything there.

My teacher used to call this whole area of confusion "The Artichoke School of Enlightenment." A person is eating an artichoke and has an awakening experience. The person concludes that the enlightenment was the result of eating the artichoke. "If only you will eat artichokes, you too can awaken."

There is nothing from a moment of expansive clarity that we can drag around to use later. "It" is gone, "I" is back. I would suggest that much of the suffering that has been inflicted by people has been caused by not understanding this principle.

SCENARIO:

The enlightened, divine master says, "Love is All."
Those around THE INDIVIDUAL WHO IS HAVING
THE EXPERIENCE are not having the experience.
They look at each other to see if anyone is
getting this.

"That means all we need to do is love," opines
one intrepid wannabe.

"That means we are love already and don't need
to do anything," theorizes
another junior master.

Soon two factions have formed (with sub-groups,
and disgruntled cliques in each faction). Hatred,
competition, antagonism, and violence grow. Ours
is the One True way. No, ours is the One True
way. All of you must die; it's what the Master
wanted. No, all of you must die; the Master has
spoken to me.

Can you picture it?

Here is what I asked the class to do:

1) Look to see what experience of expansive clarity, of insight, of intuitive knowing you have had.

2) What have you done with that experience? How has it changed you? Where does it fit into your orientation to life?

Responses

I've never told anyone about this experience since I was never quite sure of what to make of it. I also never forgot it. One day I was working in my garden. It was a pleasant day and I was about my usual routine and having a great time. I was so engrossed in it I forgot about everything else. I had my rake in my hand when all of a sudden I realized that the rake was the most perfect thing on this earth. I was enthralled with it and everything else seemed to fall into some kind of place I'd never seen or maybe realized before. It was as if everything suddenly made sense and was really OK!

I remember I began to think my way out of the experience. I decided it was endorphins or some other biochemical thing in my brain that zipped in for no good reason. I remember how nice and calming it was there.

It never happened again, but I keep looking for it. I think it was a glimpse of what the human experience is capable of. If I could "think" the experience into existence, I would have done so by now, but I can't. The frustrating thing is I know it's there somehow, outside the realm of thinking or trying. I've read mountains of stuff on satori, peak experiences, enlightenment, visions and so forth. I find them fascinating, but they are all simply beyond my "intellectual" reach, and I know that "intellectual reach" is ego saying na-na-naa-na-naa-na.

Time and again I wonder what the price is to get there and if I'm just not willing to pay it. Part of me knows the price and keeps me coming back to practice. Part of me says that it (the experience) was just an aberrant flash in the pan and it doesn't mean anything, that practice is a breath-to-breath experience with "now" being all there is. I am, as usual, befuddled. I don't know if that was an experience of expansive clarity, of insight of intuitive knowing or nothing. I wish I knew, I wish I had an answer. I don't.

I appreciate your step by step process with this, clearly expressing the various players and their viewpoints. I am fascinated with the conclusion "I am, as usual, befuddled." Maybe you are, but you had me fooled. You sounded perfectly clear to me. An "event" took place. You can't "explain" what that was. You know it was unlike anything else you've ever experienced. You watched conditioning do with it precisely what conditioning does with everything. You even know how this fits in with the rest of your life--you wish you could have it again, you know you can't make it happen. I hear no befuddlement. My encouragement is to make a deep bow, say a heartfelt thank you, and each time conditioning wants you to return to befuddlement, go instead to gratitude for having had such an unusual occurrence in your life.

I take a perfectly good insight/moment of expansive clarity and try to turn it into a belief. (Even now, I think about making a rule to stop ruining insights by turning them into beliefs.) It's not that there's anything wrong with turning an insight into a belief, its more like trying to experience something multidimensional by taking a two-dimensional snapshot of one millisecond of the process, and calling that the answer. There's nothing wrong with a snapshot as long as you remember that's all it is. When I have had moments of clarity and insight it causes a shift to happen. The entire path from that point forward is altered by that shift. My struggle to write it down, remember it, understand it, apply it, and make rules about it, feels like ego's way of trying to keep in the game and not become obsolete. The shift has already happened and all of that struggle to hold on to those insights only serves to keep me in the past and out of the present.

YES! There is nothing wrong with taking a snapshot as long as we remember that it is a snapshot. There is nothing wrong with thinking about insights, as long as we realize that we are trading the clarity of this moment for a re-hash of the last. There is no problem with any of it. When we realize we are not separate, there is no moment but the present, that lack and deprivation are illusion, one moment is no different from another, and it doesn't matter what we are doing or not doing in any of them.

It seems odd that at the moment I'm writing you about expansive moments I'm feeling quite contracted. In the past, what I've done with expansive moments is compare all other experiences to it. The result is that nothing ever quite matches up and I'm disappointed. I have an inner dialogue which goes, "If you were more.... you wouldn't be having this experience." Not a very loving voice for sure.

No, not loving, merely persistent. One day, I hope soon, you will simply tire of listening to it. It has nothing worthwhile to say and there is so much you could hear if that voice weren't drowning out the other sounds.

THIS WEEK'S assignment was short and sweet:

Here is what I asked the class to do:

Consider this statement:
"It is not possible to be afraid without holding beliefs."

Responses

I'm considering if it's possible to be afraid without holding beliefs. My mind goes quickly to all kinds of fears and lands on the BIG FEAR of dying. If I died, I think that I would be missed by my family and that my children would be sad and this scares me. But I can't prove that this would be so. I think if I was dead I might not be scared but I don't know that either. I could go on and on with this and still wind up in the same place which is "I don't know and this scares me."

I wonder if the fear of not knowing is ego fearing it's own death. It does seem that I have to hold a belief in order to be afraid. I wonder what it would be like to "free-fall" into "not knowingness" without being afraid and just being present and aware. I'd like to experience it.

I have every reason to suspect that you will experience a free-fall into not knowingness without fear, present and aware. Why would I suspect that? Because if you are seeing it, you are already experiencing it. I'm with you--I think the fear that arises with not knowing is ego fearing its own demise. If you no longer respond to the fear, if you don't go out into the future to imagine (to project) how things might be, if you are simply here, now, in this moment, ego dies. Big adrenaline rush of "fear" from egocentric karma on that one.

ENDING SUFFERING requires us to be quiet long enough to see how suffering happens. Quiet is necessary because the clamor of modern life and the endless chatter in our heads detracts from our ability to discern the automatic, conditioned, karmic patterns we mistake for who we are. This "mistake," believing ourselves to be less than we are, roars in our ears and captures our vision. As far as I know, silence is the only antidote.

This daily deluge of images and information literally rips attention away from our internal process. Completely unawares, we adopt beliefs, make assumptions, accept and reject, and generally make a dog's dinner of life. In fact, it doesn't take much looking to see that we are addicted to distraction, information, and the daily news.

DAILY NEWS
MAN BITES DOG
DOG LIVES

Here is what I asked the class to do:

Turn your attention to the information that comes to you via media--radio, television, internet, newspapers, magazines, newsletters, etc.--and look to see what is your relationship with information and believing. How much of what passes before you do you see as true? How much do you accept? What do you believe? What do you not believe? Are there certain people you automatically believe and others you automatically disbelieve? Who do you tend to accept as an authority? If you don't believe something, is it because the person is mistaken or are they lying? When you hear a report do you wonder if the facts are accurate? When do you wonder and when do you not wonder?

Please don't try to answer these questions. I'm attempting to describe the kind of fresh, open, curious mind that might explore the process of

taking in information from a new perspective
and be interested in HOW that process happens.

Responses

As a result of my engagement with the Media-Day assignment, I
stopped "my" media. Since then: no radio, no newspaper.
Being left with this new silence during my morning and evening
hours, I found out: I believe most of the information supplied to
be correct as far as the facts are concerned. I do very rarely
question these facts or see the purpose behind their delivery at
that special time.

As about 50% of the facts are those where someone else
comes to harm, I usually start my day with some catastrophic
event anywhere on the planet and am often left with the uneasy
feeling of - guilt, sometimes anger. Guilt because I am brushing
my teeth in a sheltered environment, and anger because I do
not wish this event to relate to myself. Or the flat feeling of
pure helplessness, as for example during last spring's
bombardment of Yugoslavia. Result: I am taking it ALL VERY
personally and mostly personally is associated with overcast
emotions.

Lately, the newspaper-manufacturers were on strike, an event I
would normally have taken VERY personally (no paper? where

am I being kept informed then? do they really need more money every year? why can't I do the same?...) but now I only registered this when passing the empty newsstand and thought of you: Ahh--on strike--interesting--"is that so?"

Always I encourage people simply to notice. No right. No wrong. Just notice. What happens when this? What happens when that? We're so conditioned to believe that we have to figure something out so that we will have the correct information and then we will know and then we'll be okay. If we practice noticing for a while we notice that getting the "correct information" does not make us "okay." Perceiving ourselves to be okay makes us feel okay. Period. Ironically, having more information can often leave us feeling not okay, as you have indicated. Does not listening to or reading about or watching every catastrophic (or just miserable) thing that happened anywhere on the planet mean that you don't care about people? Probably not, but I often wonder if becoming desensitized to what goes on in the world isn't the ultimate result.

I forget where the term "News Diet" originated, but it was an idea to which I readily responded. One starts with one day of not taking in any news, not reading the papers, not listening to radio and TV news, and then gradually works up to longer periods. At first there is the fear of missing out, but one soon realizes that the world does not stop, the noise is just turned down.

I wonder if this "Diet" might assist a person in becoming more "appreciative" of what news is breaking a little closer to home. Someone next door has a need and that need doesn't fall in among the other thousands, millions of needs about which I have been recently informed. Not being overwhelmed by a level of need to which I could not possibly respond, perhaps I will feel moved to act in support of my neighbor. No guarantees, but it would certainly be worth exploring.

How I respond to information is a fascinating subject to me. I am an "information scientist" by profession so I've thought about it a lot. Information is very powerful, especially when it concerns people, which it often does. It can steal my heart and mind and leave me with nothing, but I don't realize it because I'm on to the next piece of information. And each piece of it can feel so vital and important and so relevant to my life. But it's like looking at last decade's fashions. When I look back at what I was so interested in, it always seems quaint and odd and a little sad that I cared so much and thought it was such a big deal. I guess I could write a book on it, because as I think about it I get excited and go on and on to myself. But it would just be more information about information. I will let it go.

I think your analogy is excellent. How attached I was to that thing I thought I couldn't live without back then. Not that there is anything wrong with loving what we love, it's just that if I trade myself, my experience of me alive in this moment, for that thing, the cost is too dear.

It has been only recently that I find when I put my "belief" into something that I have read or heard through media or gossip, it has turned out to not be true or to not be significant enough to notice.

We hear so much nowadays about how jaded, cynical, and resigned we are as a society. People don't vote because they don't believe there's any choice. "What difference does it make? All politicians are crooks anyway." It becomes a difficult balancing act, doesn't it? On the one hand I have a lot of personal experience that many folks would say or do just about anything for a buck, yet I want to keep a high level of trust in and respect for my fellow human. I don't want to believe that everyone is working an angle or trying to pull a fast one, but each time I turn on the television or pick up a newspaper or magazine, it sure seems that there's growing evidence that honesty and integrity might be things of the past. How do we avoid these conclusions? One way is to stop getting all our information from the same types of sources.

Here is the real point for me: The world that opens up for us when we bring our attention back from all these distractions is so much more fascinating, exciting, interesting, compelling, and, yes, newsworthy than anything we'll ever find in the world of "entertainment" that, once exposed, we'll never go back. But don't take my word for it--find out for yourself.

SOMEONE FROM the class sent in the perfect lead-in for the next point I want us to explore:

Something happened a number of years ago that has continued to grab at my attention from time to time, and this exploration of beliefs and conditioning has given me a way to see it that feels helpful.

I was driving along a freeway near San Francisco, in the fast lane at evening commute time. All of a sudden the steering on my car felt really odd, and my knowledge/conditioning/belief scanner went into action, looking for what could be wrong. Ah, a flat tire! Yes! But then (and all of this happened in a matter of nano-seconds) No! It had to be more than one flat; somehow I'd gotten multiple flat tires. I turned on my signal indicators, looked back, and pleaded energetically with all the other drivers to see my plight and let me cross in front of them to the side of the road. But they weren't letting me over: "Can't you see that I've got several flat tires? I've got to get off the road!" When I was finally able to begin to pull over, I noticed that other drivers were pulling off the road too. "Whoa! We've all got flat tires. Somebody must have been ahead of us throwing nails onto the freeway." The "I" who was having this experience and believing the conclusions that the voices had reached was appalled: what a nasty, dangerous thing to do.

Finally, off the road, I got out and walked around to determine which and how many tires were flat. They were all fine. I looked up at the row of cars behind and ahead of me that were pulled off the road: lots of drivers standing outside their cars, looking bemused. Then I overheard a bit of evening news from a car radio: "...earthquake..."

Ah. Oh. Hmm. I had been so utterly convinced (here read "scammed," or "bamboozled," or "had") by the very "real" story that my Knowing One had concocted out of it's beliefs that I'd not been able to stay open to what the actual experience was.

Seeing this now, even years later, leaves me in a state of "How often during the day does a story get made up and told to me-- and believed--that is as much of a fairy tale as conditioning's explanation of my experience that day?" What a super argument for not believing any conclusions, any stories, anything!!

Here is what I asked the class to do:

Please consider the following:
What in your life did you at one time believe utterly and subsequently found yourself not believing at all?

Responses

Up until the "There's Nothing Wrong With You" retreat in January, I was buying into the one, scrawny voice that was convincing me I have no more reason to live, this is all so stupid, let's find a creative way to end it all, like a weird car accident. Since the retreat, I am more interested in amplifying that lame voice, having a bit of a row with it, and feeling so alive that I wouldn't check out of this planet until I get a few more rounds with that pest!

I am alive, I am okay with it, I am breathing, I am wondering who the heck "I" am, and we are all seeming to have a pretty darned good time at this. Thanks.

I can see you lacing up those gloves, stepping

into the ring, dancing around throwing those warm up punches, having the time of your life, and egocentric conditioning (who was recently so very robust in its arguments for your demise) is over in the corner whining about not feeling so good.

Now for anyone who is concerned that I am advocating violent abuse of egocentric conditioning, please note that I did not suggest going over and pummeling ego as it whines. It is just good to have a chance to be generous from a position of power.

Despite the fact of doing a fair bit of paying attention, believing as little as possible, and trying not to take any of it personally, it appears I was missing quite a bit! I've always been aware that I go through mood swings at work; alternating between finding it a tolerable way to earn a living and a life energy sucking source of misery. But I'd never really had a clue as to the source of the problem. Mostly I assumed that I didn't like the job very much, and the mood swings just played down or amplified the situation.

But the other day I was feeling really low at work. And it occurred to me that I must be believing something to feel that low down. So I paid lots of attention to what was going on and was really surprised at my findings: a little boy who felt so bad about himself and thought that anyone could see how defective he was. Actually I even felt like I smelled bad, and if people got close enough for a whiff, they'd be totally disgusted! Now, I have no idea if any of this relates to a particular childhood experience, something involving toilet training perhaps, but I know that as an adult, I don't smell bad. Yet here I was, totally buying into this very bad feeling that I wasn't even aware of until that moment.

This wasn't the first time I'd contacted core feelings of defectiveness, but I keep thinking that the years of therapy and meditating had gotten me past it. I was just about to write that I felt bad to find these feelings still there, but that's taking it personally, isn't it? I guess the best I can do is to pay attention to these feelings when they come up at work and try to support the scared little boy who feels that bad about himself. It's hard to support him when I don't even know he's there. It's also hard to pay attention to him because I feel so identified with his feelings at the time. I hope all the messages of these classes and the support of this great online Sangha will help see me through.

You are my "paying attention" hero. What you have described is IT. That is the process, the practice, of letting suffering go. Here is the only thing I would ask you to consider: You will never be finished.

Egocentricity will groan as if that's bad news, but it will only be going for dramatic effect. It doesn't want suffering to end BECAUSE IT IS SUFFERING. When suffering ends, egocentricity ends. Trust me, complain as it might about never being free of suffering, it is wiping its little brow in relief that it will live to suffer another day.

Here is one of the great, joyous, brilliant paradoxes of life: If you want to be free of suffering, you must embrace suffering.

I ask you to sit still (since obviously this is something you do) with those two notions. 1) As long as you live, there will be suffering that arises to be resolved, whether it is an authentic wound to be embraced and healed or conditioning to let go,

142

and 2) the only way not to suffer is to be willing to suffer.

One other suggestion: It can be helpful not to wait for karma to present itself, but rather to go into the day actively looking for its appearance. In your case, this means TAKING that little boy to  work rather than waiting for him to show up hoping you will recognize him before great misery ensues.

It may sound simplistic, BUT I believe I'm separate and I am afraid. Period. All the rest of it seems to come out of that, all the permutations and details and ways to deal with that belief make up all the rest. I am aware of this in a gut level way, not just jargon regurgitated. Suddenly I am aware of "me," and there is Mom all the way across the room absorbed in something other than me, and there's all this DISTANCE between me and that comfort, love, food, warmth, security and I am afraid. Bottom line. After all, I can't see the air that's there connecting us in that space between. I've relived this again and again and again, only the form "Mom" takes keeps changing.

This has nothing to do with theory, does it? We talk (endlessly!) about the illusion of a separate self as the cause of suffering, and now what that means is, as you say, felt in the gut. But before addressing that specifically, I want to take a moment to speak to the process of that realization because it says so much about the "how" of awareness practice. This "how" is the same in many other walks of life; we just don't realize that it applies in awareness practice as well.

The person who is guiding you in the steps of expanding awareness is constantly describing what is just beyond your current ability to see. You take a step, and the guide describes the next place you will be putting a foot down. You take that step, and as you are balanced there, the next step is described. You put your foot down. In this way you safely move from where you are to where you want to be. (Interestingly, that "where you want to be" is exactly where you began, but that's another story.)

The person guiding you is not going to put your foot down for you. You must do that for yourself. But the description about how, when, and where will be very complete. It may take a while as you're balanced and poised, listening to the directions and figuring out exactly what they mean, but sooner or later, you'll get it and be able to put the foot down confidently. As the trip progresses, placing the feet gets easier and quicker. Confidence builds. No more does it feel like random, confusing, conflicting pieces of unrelated information. As indicated in an earlier response, the process becomes crystal clear.

However, crystal clear does not necessarily mean comfortable or pleasant. The new view may be something you've been avoiding seeing for lifetimes. Again, if waking up were easy and pain-free, the process would be much more popular.

So here you are seeing that you, in fact, FEEL separate, and you are, in fact, afraid. The good news is that you don't have to panic because it seems that the tools you used to get to this place no longer work where you are now. They do work. The same tools that got you to this view will serve you well in going beyond this view and making your way to the next view.

What are those tools, you may ask, since one of the reactions to the sudden siting of the edge of a precipice is loss of memory. Let's go through them together. Where do you feel separate? What is it (in body, feelings, mind, or mind objects) that signals "separation"? How do you know that signal means that? In your example you indicated that Mom is clear across the room absorbed in something other than you. Does physical distance always mean separation? Do you ever feel connected yet have physical space between you and the "other"? HOW is this phenomenon occurring?

When you finish looking at that, I want you to tackle fear. Begin, please, with how that signal means (in this instance) that you must call what you feel "fear," and how do you know that feeling means all you have attached to it?

I could ask you questions endlessly, but you know what I'm pointing at. Lots of beliefs, assumptions, unexamined habits and conditioning going on here. Who believes all this, how does it remain unexamined, and who has an investment in not seeing how all of this works?

The Third Key

Don't
take
anything
personally

AS HUMAN BEINGS we have the ability to perceive ourselves as separate. Our minds are able to remember and discriminate. We can recall ourselves in situation after situation over time, thinking, feeling, moving, and interacting. It seems reasonable and logical that there is a constant "someone" who is the actor, the experiencer in life. Even as we age and must admit there is nothing about us that is exactly the same as in youth, we cling to the belief that there is a constant "I" who has this awareness.

One of the fundamental questions in Zen is "Who am I?" We can also legitimately phrase that question, "Who is I?" or even, "What is I?" The master asking this question is attempting to get the student to find that constant "I." The not very well kept secret is that the master is actually attempting to guide the student toward a realization that there is no such thing as a constant, continuous, "I" (or anything else) that is separate from and in a subject/object relationship with life.

That which believes itself to be separate, the egocentric survival system that childhood social conditioning produces (often referred to as ego) is in a desperate battle to maintain itself against the perceived threat that life is. For ego, each moment of life is a threat to its survival. Egocentricity does not feel at home. It believes itself to be separate from life, in opposition to life, attempting to get what it wants and needs in spite of life. Ego takes everything in life very personally!

We, as egocentric separate selves, take life personally because as children we were taught to take it personally. Childhood social conditioning relies heavily on reward and punishment as means of eliciting "acceptable" behavior. If you don't eat your vegetables, you can't have dessert. If you don't do your chores, you can't ride your bike. When you get a little older, you are grounded. Freedom of movement, communication, and friendship are taken away if you "misbehave." Not getting what you want is punishment and losing what you have is punishment, while getting what you want is proof that you are good and deserve reward. We conclude that it is all very, very personal. I am good when I... I am bad when I... I should feel this... I shouldn't feel that... I am this... I am not that...

HERE ARE SOME dictionary definitions of "personal":

1. Belonging to human beings, not to things or abstractions.

2. Pertaining to or characteristic of a person, or self-conscious being.

3. Private, individual, affecting individuals, peculiar or proper to a certain person.

Here is what I asked the class to do:

What is your experience of "taking it personally"?

Responses

Taking something personally can be summed up in four words, "It's all about me." Whether it's a comment spoken, an event or happenstance I am witnessing, or even the current state of the world, the conditioned response is, "What does this mean for me? How will this affect me? What did he/she mean (about me) when he/she said that?" What tremendous relief and sweetness there is to slip into not being me. A quote I find helpful is, "Your little ego can only hurt my little ego. Ha! Ha!" I have taken that insight with me into many a discussion.

At the airport flying home from a retreat, I waited in line as a distressed woman, who had barged in front of me, harangued the agent about having received an incorrect gate assignment. He tried hard to help her, but she just turned on her heel, as he was mid-sentence, and stormed off down the corridor. He shook his head, gave me a rueful smile and said, "Everyone is a victim. You know, brain surgery is serious. Gate changes are not serious." A wise man. How easily we lose sight of the fact that it is just our little egos flexing their little muscles. The "Ha! Ha!" helps keep the perspective.

When I take something personally, I am usually assuming it is about me before I know that is true.

I was talking with a woman recently who, after

struggling all her life to come to terms with how she was treated as a child at the hands of neglectful, abusive parents, suddenly "got it" that what happened to her was not personal at all! This can sound outrageous until we see, as she did, that those two people would have treated ANY child as they treated her. They didn't treat her the way they did because she was who she was. They were too unconscious to have any idea who she was. That was the whole point--- they barely knew she existed! For it to be personal it would have had to involve her and she realized it did not. How liberating. Now we're working to be liberated by the awareness that nothing except our own conditioning is doing anything to us.

My experience with taking things personally has to do with seeing myself as the center of the universe. In this mode nothing really exists unless it in some way has something to do with me.

Just recently (and I do believe, thanks to the looking encouraged by this class) I've experienced a breakthrough with a couple of people toward whom I've been trying to feel loving but whose behavior kept irritating me. Despite my best efforts, on a subliminal level I was pulling away from them and closing down. Suddenly it's as if I can see into their hearts without ME being there stomping around and asking, "What about ME?" It's such an incredibly expansive feeling I think my heart is literally opening.

I love that image: "Suddenly it's as if I can see into their hearts without ME being there stomping around and asking, 'What about ME?'" Gosh, I wonder why other people don't want us to be the center of their universe? Could it be the same reason we don't want them at the center of ours? How amazing to see people, even for the tiniest glimpse of a moment, as the center of their own lives. What an irony that the same process that fears and despises separation while believing separation to be the "truth" of reality, cannot imagine anyone as actually separate from itself.

With this exercise I wanted to PROVE how what happens to us in life IS personal. I am surprised to hear myself say that the gesture that came to me was to bow to the place in me that knows that taking things personally is absolutely different from having a personal experience. And that in this gesture of bowing lies forgiveness for all of us.

And, we can take that one giant step further: There is no "you," there is no "I," there is only "us." There is only a "we" that is "all" from which no thing is separate.

It is much too large a concept to understand, even if it weren't for the fact that in attempting to understand, we are trying to grasp that which contains us. Not possible. In a flash of intuitive clarity, we can sense the inseparable nature of all life, but we cannot GRASP it. The process of becoming someone who is going to grasp it eliminates our ability to BE "nonseparation."

Some people use the word GOD to attempt to point at the circle with no remainder, the ALL from which no thing is other. If we used that word, we could express what we're trying to see in this way: God is driving down the freeway, God cuts God off, God is scared, God is oblivious to

God's fear, God gets angry, God wants revenge, God steals God from God, God lies to God. If we have trouble with the word GOD, we could use PINK or THING or whatever word we choose to represent ALL THIS. If for a split second we can "see" this, we can know that even a "personal" experience is not possible. Not because there is no experience, but because there is no "me."

 I had been paying close attention to this class, but now I have a major distraction: a girlfriend. Suddenly I am filled with desire to have her in my life, and I'm taking it very personally. I want her for me! I can't think straight about this. It's as if all my meditation experience and learning flew out the window. I feel I can't be complete without her, but the teachings say I am complete already, right? Is self-hate telling me that I need this person to make me whole?

Well, I don't know. It is an intense lesson in what the Buddha taught though, isn't it? The interesting part in this to me is that we get confused about which part is which. People (conditioning) will conclude that what Buddhism teaches is that if you're going to be a spiritual person you can't fall in love or want someone in your life. Nothing could be further from the truth. The Buddha merely encouraged us to consider, closely and carefully, how going unconscious and acting out of the greed, hate, and delusion of karma can lead to suffering. Ego would very much like us to conclude that awareness practice and falling in love are mutually exclusive. In fact, falling in love can be a real workshop! What doesn't work well together is unconsciousness and awareness practice. Keep us posted.

Recently I was talking to a good friend about something I was taking personally and feeling cranky about. I started to defend my position, telling her of past incidents that reinforced my fears of impending doom, when I suddenly heard myself nattering away, and I was mortified. I stopped mid-sentence and, embarrassed, muttered, "Yeah, that's my story, and I'm sticking to it." My friend looked me in the eye and said, "No, that's your story, and it's sticking to you." That seemed like the most delightful thing I had ever heard! I saw myself covered with those tiny little post-it notes, which I could peel off and read one at a time--all the beliefs, all the justifications, all the slights, all the imperfections, all the reasons why the world wasn't the way it should be. HA HA HA! My ego is a petty little bureaucrat who tries to run things from a tiny, dank little office with no windows!

The Buddha suggested to us that we can take refuge in the three jewels, Bodhi (awakening), Dharma (the teachings), and Sangha (those who practice). He seemed to feel each was of equal importance and none can be left out without great loss. Your little tale beautifully demonstrates how and why this is so: helpful awareness, helpful insight, helpful friend.

One way I take things personally is by identifying with the voice that says there is too much to do so I better do those things and skip sitting—all because if certain things don't get done, it says something about me. I've watched this often, but something new I noticed this time is the physical fatigue and lassitude I feel around the time I return to daily sitting. That may be what triggers the willingness to disidentify and return to a sitting schedule. It also is fuel for conditioning to try to get me to sleep a little later! Seeing this stuff is a lot of fun and energizing.

It is fun, isn't it? IF WE DON'T TAKE ANY OF IT PERSONALLY! The voices say this, the voices say that. Okay. Voices all over the world are saying all sorts of nonsense all the time. Seems to be a big part of what

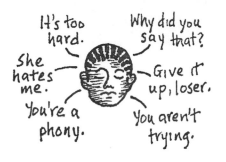

It's too hard.
She hates me.
You're a phony.
Why did you say that?
Give it up, loser.
You aren't trying.

voices do. Do I really need to take THESE voices personally? Do I really need to get miserable when a voice has an opinion about what I'm doing? Who is that voice? Why do I prioritize that opinion? Why do I believe that voice is more right, meaningful, or important than the voice of someone who loves me? It is fun just to watch. I can love going to a baseball game if I am just there to watch great athletes do what they do best on a sunny day. If how "my" team performs sets the tone for the rest of my week, if I am miserable when they lose, then it can be big drama for egocentricity, but it's not "fun." Fun happens with disidentification and not taking things personally.

Yesterday an old familiar feeling of depression came over me. Immediately, I started trying to figure out what was going on, what I needed to do to stop feeling that way. When I read this assignment, I realized it had never occurred to me not to take depression personally. I can see that resisting the feelings just maintained them.

I feel that some part of me needs to be taken care of during those times. Is that an egocentric thought? I suddenly feel like crying as I write this. There seems to be a profound sadness...the loss of some needed assurance of other people's love, and when it's not there I feel like I don't belong. I guess at least I'm seeing that I'm taking it all personally. But where is the freedom? And now I'm angry that whoever (ego?) would use such grief, of such a little person, to maintain suffering. Oh, here we go again!

I go to the Indianapolis 500 and find myself feeling depressed, joyless, without love. I hate this feeling. I don't want to be feeling this way. Why am I feeling this? I'm here to have fun. But the cars just keep going around and around and I feel depressed. What is this about? Oh, it's that car in the back. That car isn't going fast enough, isn't winning. Poor little car. Poor, poor little car! Why are they treating that car that way? Why are they not letting the poor little car win? I hate them! I hate them all! I hate myself for hating them! I hate everyone at the race watching the poor little car get beaten. Why am I feeling this way? Why can't I stop feeling this?

Here are the important pieces of that little tale: 1) The cars just keep going around the track. 2) Snacks are available. 3) You can leave any time. 4) You can actually be there present to the whole event instead of sitting in the stands hating it.

The "here we go again" is actually good news--we have lots and lots of opportunities to see how we cause ourselves to suffer and lots of opportunities to make another choice.

Yesterday I needed to pay an income tax installment but had misplaced the piece of paper that tells who I am and how much I owe. I called and asked how I could pay without the piece of paper and was told it could probably be handled at the bank. But the bank said I had to have the piece of paper after all. I found myself angry. Then I became aware that I was taking it personally, and I tried to understand why. It was simply because "I" did not get my way. It did not matter that I knew the deadline was coming up and I had procrastinated; "I" did not get my way, "I" took it personally, and "I" was angry. Amazing!

Life is always supposed to say "yes" to me and I get to say "no" to life. When it doesn't go that way, "I" am angry. How dare life not do what I want?! Sounds very like a toddler, doesn't it? Years ago I read a psychologist who opined that we never develop emotionally beyond the age of four. I thought she was being generous---we so rarely get out of the "terrible" twos!

Last night I was playing a game with my son, expressly for the purpose of learning how to play. He became frustrated and sad that he was not going to win the practice game, even though we had tied no stakes to winning. Because he felt bad, I began to feel bad, thinking I must have done something wrong. At first I tried to talk to him about it, then I realized that I was taking his loss very personally—I wanted to protect him from feeling bad. Oddly enough, he spoke less about that game than other losses he had suffered when playing games against his friends. I saw that (my projections, of course) "losing" means for him that he is "less than" the winner, and his experience of losing overshadows triumphs he's had and forgotten (not just in winning, but in learning). It gave me ideas for ways that I could be with him and talk with him to help ease his pain about losses without my suffering his hurts too much. I say that because I think one of the hardest things a parent has to endure is his/her own child's suffering—which leads me to ponder, How do parents not take reactions of their child personally? Does it come back to the illusion of separation?

So much suffering exists in the world because we take our "own" children personally and not "other" children. I just read the statistic that 24,000 people starve to death each day, 75% of which are children. That's one person every 3.6 seconds, one child every 4.8 seconds. I wonder what would be possible if we all decided to make that the thing we take personally.

Could we model for children something such as playing as hard as one can play, harder than one thought it possible to play, and finding the enjoyment in the playing rather than in the "winning"? Could we raise children with an awareness of "others" that allowed the child to play all-out and have no interest in keeping score? How about a child who is secure enough and generous enough to want an "other," to whom it is still important, to feel triumph? I think all that is quite possible, but what is required is for us to first resolve these issues within ourselves.

These perspectives will result in a far happier life for our children than any amount of "winning," or even learning how to be all right "losing."

I have been going along in this course, reading and paying attention while I'm reading but not really doing much noticing any other time. But these last couple of days have been exciting for me as I've returned to active noticing. And today I really got a good look at the endless stream of abuse I've been getting from ego. It's awful! It is nonstop! What a total bunch of craziness! I saw very vividly the game you described where no matter what I do, ego wins and I lose. And none of the beating makes any sense at all. The games ego plays, the justifications it uses, are basically nuts. Wow.

I find your observation about the difference between noticing and not noticing powerful. That process keeps me (and many, many others in similar lines of work) in business. I wouldn't mind at all if that process collapsed and I could spend more of the day watching the trees grow.

All around us are volumes of information that tell us paying attention, noticing, being present, living here, living now is the secret to ending suffering. We don't do it. We FORGET! There is a killer roaming the streets in your neighborhood and you forget. You forget to lock the door! Astounding. Truly amazing. But almost everyone lives life just like that.

You've seen it. Don't forget. Do whatever it takes not to forget.

MANY RESPONSES to the first exercise regarding "taking things personally" mentioned being "the center of the universe" in the sense of "everything relates to me." It is intriguing that most, if not all, of us also are mired in what I call self-hate. Anne Lamott, in *Traveling Mercies*, refers to this as being "the piece of sh-t at the center of the universe."

Here is what I asked the class to do:

If this seems so for you, what is your experience of ego's vacillation between "I am everything-numero uno-the cog around which life revolves (center of the universe)" and "I am nothing-unworthy-a loser (self-hate)"?

SELF HATE

CENTER OF THE UNIVERSE

Responses

In my experience of ego's ping-ponging between being the greatest and being the worst, there is always a hint of "I'm not worthy" sitting around waiting to pounce at any opportunity. I can be feeling just great about my life, but I have an internal scanner who always looks for loopholes and ways to remind me of how "less than" I really am. The scanner can ruin all kinds of enjoyable situations. It's at full speed when I am at work. In social situations, it can twist the most innocent comment into something that shows me how unworthy I am. It can even interpret silence!

What you have articulated is how conditioning wins regardless of the placement of the ball in this ping-pong match of karma. You do well, you're happy, no problem; you can always be threatened with the future. You're having a hard time (and would you be having a hard time without the constant yammer of conditioned voices?) and egocentricity is having a field day.

It is a funny game (in a pathetic sort of way). Can you imagine this in football? Two teams come out on the field and one of them scores a touchdown. The other team gets the ball and scores a touchdown, but the first team gets the points. Throughout the game, regardless of which team scores, the first team gets the points. If this were like our life with karmic conditioning, every time something happens, the first team would always score and the other team never would! Something happens, ego scores and I lose. Every time.

In football, people would get tired of it and quit playing. We get tired of it, but rarely does anyone quit playing.

When I feel trapped in a problem, there is a sense of constriction in my belief that others involved are concerned only with my response. In a relationship, I imagine that the other person is just waiting for me to act.

When I feel unworthy, I'm scared, I'm small right in the middle of my solar plexus. A rush of energy, a falling feeling: I'm not worthy to act from how I feel, I must act in a way that will not cause pain to others. Others, then, are more worthy than I. I am their subordinate. Oh, this makes me angry to write and yet I so often believe this to be true, or think and act as if it is.

What you're doing is very much like what we do with "process mapping." I do this, then I feel this, then I say that, then that happens, then I feel this, etc. As you go through it in this way you begin to see where the "lies" are hidden in the form of assumptions and unexamined beliefs. As you see this for what it is, the constrictions begin to loosen and you have greater freedom.

It seems to me it is all about fear and staying stuck in the fear. If I'm #1 in the universe, I become fearful that I will lose that status. This leads to feeling "I am nothing-unworthy-a loser" because I can't maintain the #1 feeling. I then go to fear that I am losing control over my life and am compelled to run out and recreate that #1 feeling again.

If I am following this experience—watching how I go from super-person-of-the-universe to dirt--it shows me how my thoughts keep me in a fearful circle. I have discovered through mindfulness that if I just watch it, I'm not jerked either way.

Precisely so. At the end of this book I make a suggestion about what is available when one is no longer being jerked back and forth from one side of a duality to the other. A hint: Joy is what is present when we stop doing everything else.

Currently I'm taking some comfort in watching myself go off center and incorporating those incidents as part of my sense of self, sort of revising my self-image with a lower standard. It's a temporary relief. But I am aware that this is a stop-gap measure with another layer beneath it. And another beneath that, and another. All these revised selves are more of the same process. So, what's valuable now is to be looking at THAT process, open to what will be revealed next.

I am going to quote you everywhere and often. "Revising my self-image with a lower standard." I hope everyone can see how beneficial that would be. Each time I revise the self-image egocentricity has adopted as a survival tool, I include more and more of life in the things-that-are-like-me and ways-that-I-am-too category. If I keep going long enough, nothing will be excluded. Oneness.

WE LIVE IN a world of infinite possibility. As humans, we have the ability to experience ourselves as separate from that and then cling to that separation, all the while decrying our loneliness and isolation and suffering terribly in the process. We search everywhere for relief, but we fail to notice that <u>the illusion of separation is conducting the search</u>, and it has no interest in oneness and connection and possibility.

This world of possibility is available to us through the practice of conscious compassionate awareness.

Here are some things that are possible:

1) Not to take offense

My teacher would say, "We are as much a pain in the neck when we take offense as when we give offense." It is not possible to control whether or not we give offense. If we lived in a constant state of enlightened, unconditional compassion, we couldn't keep people from being offended by what we might say or do.

2) Not to be defensive

If we truly want to end suffering, we will realize
that the only thing that wants to be defended is
egocentric, karmic conditioning, and we will not
want to defend that.

3) Not to have different standards for
yourself and others

This can be expressed as neither being
unaccepting of something in myself that I have
no problem with in someone else, nor being
intolerant of something in someone else that I
allow in myself. I go to work regardless of the
way I feel, but encourage others to take care
of themselves when they're sick. I tell you a
"little white lie" to extricate myself from a social
situation, but feel hurt and upset if I discover
you've responded to an invitation from me in
the same way.

4) Not to take your up-bringing any more

personally than you would take that of a stranger

My behavior can be explained, justified, and excused by my family history; you should meet my standards of behavior regardless of what happened to you.

5) Not to take personally the thoughts in your head or the feelings in your body

If "I" is an illusion of separation, how can anything, including thoughts and feelings, be owned as "mine"?

6) Not to take personally your conditioned opinion of yourself

There's a book titled, "Your Opinion of Me Is None of My Business." We could easily extend that to "My (conditioning's) opinion of me is none of my business."

176

7) Not to take your karma personally

I have no awareness of having made choices about who I am, what I look like, my level of intelligence, my gender, my family, my childhood, my race, my health, my social milieu, etc. There are those who would argue that these are my choices, but I don't know that and see no reason to take it up as a belief.

Here is what I asked the class to do:

Look and see how, or if, these apply to your life.

Responses

Not to have different standards for yourself and others hits home, but I'm not sure I understand it. For example, I don't have a problem with seeing smoking cigarettes and drinking alcohol as unacceptable in myself whereas it doesn't bother me that someone else does those things. Please help, as I am new to this practice.

Well, you're off to a good start. You have noticed something about how you are. You accomplished that through paying attention. You're open to seeing how this "inconsistency" (of having different standards) works. Now the practice is to continue to pay attention until you see in a moment of clarity HOW you hold that process in place. You will see what you believe, how you have been conditioned, how a conditioned belief is held in the body, all the beliefs that must be held in place to keep the whole structure together, the fear that is behind the structures, etc. Soon the practice of seeing will be much more interesting than the practice of holding unexamined structures in place, the structures will begin to dissolve through the seeing, and you will begin to experience a truly compelling freedom.

Just keep noticing.

I remember two instances at work when I felt compelled to give people feedback about some aspect of their behavior that had annoyed me. In one case, I felt the person made unkind comments about work I'd done and had been rude to another person, both of which I took personally. Usually when I feel attacked, I try to put some time and space between me and the incident, but I was motivated by my sense of "rightness" and wanting to get things taken care of right away. I tried to be diplomatic about how I gave the feedback, the response was extreme defensiveness on the part of the recipients. I found myself struggling to keep the conversation focused on what I'd intended to say and getting defensive myself as they counterattacked. After both incidents, I found myself in my office with the door closed, my head on my desk, knowing that I had handled things very badly and wondering how wanting to do "good" could cause so much aggravation.

My relationship with those folks afterwards remained just civil enough to get work done. I only spoke to them when I absolutely had to, because I was fearful of stirring up bad feelings again. Even now, when I think of those incidents the discomfort comes back in my gut.

So I'm noticing as I write this that besides making assumptions and judgments, believing things I probably shouldn't have, and then taking things personally, I'm still beating myself up for these incidents, hearing somewhat faintly, "You should have known better". Ouch—time for turning compassion inward.

Urgency. Urgency is the devil's henchman. Urgency is egocentricity's greatest ally. And it got you, didn't it? It's painful! It is also how we learn. So, you've seen it. That thrust of urgency hits you, the righteous indignation, Crusader Rabbit to the rescue, and off you go to take those steps that are going to lead you to your  head down on your desk, feeling like garbage, with a trail of wrecked relationships behind you. But what to do? Is the only other choice a diet of bile? No. Here again, we get to practice paying attention. That's why I find even the most disastrous of interactions to be profitable--you get to see what's going on. Next time you feel that ire rise up perhaps you will recall these situations. Perhaps a little light will turn on in conscious awareness and you will tune in more attentively. What are the voices saying? What are you assuming? What are you believing? What are you ignoring? What is the relationship between the energy and the voices? What do you believe about emotion at this pitch? How do you know: that you're right, that the other person is who you see him to be, that what you're about to do will help, that you (or anyone) will feel better after, that another course of action might not be better? If you really pursue this line of questioning, you will learn so much from the questioning that you may lose all interest in further action. You may just walk by the "bad guy," give him a very large and genuine smile, and say, "thank you!" Most of us, not knowing why we're getting that big smile and thank you, but assuming we deserve it (!) will just smile back and feel good. Not a bad contribution to make to the world.

For me, taking things personally is my way of defending what I hold sacred, what I think should be given a certain level of attention or care or respect: myself, my family, my home, my feelings, my friends' feelings. Why do I have to defend these things from disrespect? Why do I think they need to be kept sacred? Because I fear the world that would exist if they were not. This is based on the assumption that there is actually something I can do to defend these things, or that someone else can harm them, or that they exist at all. I assume that a world without respect for things like life and spirit would be painful.

I would agree that a world without respect for things like life and spirit would be painful--it is. But here's what strikes me about that: We all have a different version of what is worthy of respect and of what represents life and spirit, and we're all fighting to have ours respected while failing to respect others'. Hence the breakdown. I'm not going to respect you and yours if you don't respect me and mine. But no one bothers to find out what that means! We just assume, project, and take offense. We assume intent where there is only ignorance. I sometimes wonder if our attachment is more to righteousness than to life and spirit.

"Not to have different standards for yourself and others." The more I look at this one, the more I find that I have totally different standards for myself and for others. I admire and praise artistic work and people who take creative risks, but I avoid risks at all cost. In fact, I feel burning envy of people who paint or photograph or write, but I cling to my office job and make sure not to do anything that would prevent the paycheck from coming at the end of the week. "I've got to support my family, don't I?"

I'm intolerant of people who are intolerant. Well, at least this one has become obvious enough to me that I actually pay attention and see a change.

I've been trying to picture meeting myself face to face and giving myself the advice (or holding myself to the standard that I hold others). I see two people who apparently look alike talking right past each other, both thinking, "Man, I can't wait to get away from this weirdo!" —two complete strangers meeting inside of me, both baffled by who let the other guy in. Very funny. I'm not sure what to do with these two jokers...

Your image of the two identical people, talking right past each other, both thinking, "man, I can't wait to get away from this weirdo," will stay with me. Such a graphic picture of what the conditioned world is up against, inside and out. I see someone who is exactly like a part of me I have been conditioned to hate, and I hate that person, never having a clue that I hate them BECAUSE they are like me. I see someone who is not like me and feel insecure and inferior in their presence, having no clue that I feel insecure and inferior BECAUSE I am like them and have been conditioned to deny my own adequacy.

Often I marvel that the world is in as good a shape as it is and that we haven't managed to annihilate ourselves.

This feels like totally new information to me, totally new ways to consider! I feel my mind and body trying to grasp the meanings of these possibilities.

The idea to not take personally my karma, my conditioned opinion of myself, the thoughts in my head or feelings in my body, or my upbringing is just mind-boggling. How do I do that? Where do I even begin? The idea of being free from what goes on in my head sounds very appealing...not being controlled by it sounds peaceful.

I think of this practice as "getting comfortable on roller skates in a room full of ball bearings." You have to learn to enjoy the thrill of those first 10 seconds on a roller coaster! Once we learn to feel that "weeeeeeee" as joy rather than terror, the thrills come fast and furious. It gets scary only when we try to slam on the brakes.

How do you do all this? You're doing it. Just don't quit.

The idea of "Don't take it personally" is certainly not limited to Zen, as it's something we hear all the time. That's why I thought this would be one of the simplest lessons. It's turned into the most difficult, though, because it's where self-hate doubles up on itself. It slips out of its spot to attack the place where it was from a different position.

The other day at work, I had several coffee drinks to make at once. A man who had just ordered a drink saw me making another person's drink, assumed it was his, and yelled at me for not making the drink the way he wanted. My concentration was broken, I was upset, and I was taking it awfully personally!

After that, I decided I wanted to be alone, so I volunteered to wash dishes, away from the crowds of people. As I washed, I fumed. How rude! Then I thought of the lesson, "Don't take it personally," but it came from such a wrong and twisted place. "Come on! You know better than that. Don't take it personally! Can't you get it? If some jerk wants to yell at you when you're doing your job, that's his problem, not yours! You shouldn't be paying attention to him! Aren't you better than that? Stop taking it personally! Stop this very minute!"

The voice of conditioning can be scary. It's so stuck there that it thinks it can will itself away, and it can't. I think of an acting class I took in which one of my fellow students had trouble showing confidence. Every time she did something that called for correction, she apologized profusely. Eventually the teacher asked, "Please stop apologizing!" And the student said, "I'm sorry."

How do you stop apologizing for apologizing? How do you stop feeling guilty about your guilt? How do you stop from taking "Don't take it personally" personally?

You always hear people say, "Please don't take this personally"—why do they never say, "Please take this personally?"

The way we stop apologizing for apologizing, stop feeling guilty about feeling guilty and stop "taking it personally" personally is through conscious, compassionate awareness. We don't have to do anything to make anything stop. If we simply pay attention, if we just quietly observe, then how the suffering is held in place will be revealed, and we will stop doing what we are doing to hold it in place. It will simply fall away. We're doing that here, together, now.

I think we should start a "please take this personally" campaign. Before each compliment (which could be plentiful and always true) we say, "Please take what I am about to tell you personally." There are those who would jump immediately to the other side of the duality and say, "But I thought you said there was no one to take anything personally!" It would be worth the exercise just to help people make that leap and let them know they can do it. In my experience people don't like to let something go before they've "had" it completely. Perhaps a helpful step in not taking the "negative" personally is to take the "positive" personally. I am for anything that mixes things up. Above all, let's not stay stuck.

The Seventh Possible Thing, not to take your karma personally, is huge for me. It seems to encompass the other Six Possible

Things. If I understand what you are pointing at, it means it is possible to take absolutely nothing personally. The stuff that is most uniquely "me," isn't. My deepest fears, worst failings, greatest talents, most profound loves, pet peeves aren't "mine." Even the ability to experience an "I" who takes things personally doesn't have to be taken personally.

You understand what I am pointing at PERFECTLY. A fabulous koan, if I do say so myself!

Not to take personally thoughts and feelings: Can the same be applied to physical pain? I tend to identify strongly with physical pain. When I'm feeling pain, the pain IS me. If I take out the thoughts that go with the pain, what would be left? Just pain? Pain without meaning? Could my mind/ego possibly accept pain without meaning? My mind wants to "understand" the pain, make sense of it, know its origin, its past, its future, in order to control it. Can I let the pain be uncontrollable (which it is anyway)? Maybe this is part of not taking my karma personally.

It is a part of a "Buddhist view" (if there could be such a thing), to see pain as THE pain, rather than MY pain. Pain is. Life is painful. We have these fragile bodies. These fragile bodies are

given to injury and deterioration. When these
bodies are injured or deteriorate, we experience
that change as pain. None of this is personal.
No body has been born that didn't or won't
experience old age, sickness, and death. The
difficulty we face is, in spite of great evidence
to the contrary, no one actually accepts that
these laws of life apply to them! We understand
all this in theory, but when that hair starts
falling out, or those bulges appear, or the
wrinkles become undeniable, it is a shock. We
take our body for granted when it is performing
as it "should," and we resent it when it doesn't
act as we wish. None of which results in facing
an obvious reality: bodies have a life of their
own. (Or perhaps it would be clearer to say
bodies have a karma of their own.)

"Not to take personally the thoughts in your head or the
feelings in your body." I'm not sure what that means. I
paraphrased it for myself as not taking thoughts and feelings
too seriously. That is, I don't decide that they mean something
and that I must do something about them. I can notice them
and recognize that all thoughts and feelings are just passing
through.

"Not to take personally your conditioned opinion of yourself."
Again, to understand it better, I would paraphrase this as
follows: if I think I'm a good person or a bad person or
deserving or stupid or clever or whatever the judgment, it's a
sure path to suffering to give that any credibility, to feel that it's
true IN ANY WAY.

This exercise of rephrasing the statements was for myself, so I
could absorb them better and notice the times when I do and
don't do all those things.

Seems to me that "rephrasing" or paraphrasing
can be a very helpful tool, and I would encourage
you to continue to look. Often we feel better
when we position something so we can "understand" it, but often understanding is merely
putting something in a form that conditioning can
integrate. So much of what we're talking about
in this class is designed to throw people out of
their conditioned orientation to life, maximizing
the possibility of one of those moments of
intuitive sensing or clarity. I like to just back-
burner these kinds of things, and sort of circle
around them. Bring them forward periodically
for a fresh view.

Years ago I read Zen Flesh, Zen Bones, and understood all the words that were in English (or thought I did), and that was about the extent of it. What those people were talking about was incomprehensible to me, though I loved reading the book. I have read it regularly over the years and each time I've read it, I realize a little more is clear to me. How has that clarity happened? I've continued an awareness practice, and as my awareness increases, what is being pointed at in the book becomes more available to me. It's like reading a map and a tour book and then going to the place. Reading the map and the tour book AFTER you've visited somewhere is a completely different experience from the reading one does before. One is theory, the other is practice.

I am stuck on the seventh possibility and need help with the concept of karma. If "I" is the illusion of separation and there is no individual "self", does karma operate only on the level of the collective self?

I want to do a whole class (and a book) on

karma, because it is a huge subject. Time and space demand that this be the short answer to your question. As far as I can tell, karma is nothing more than a concept that allows us humans to believe we know something about a life that is incomprehensible to us. We look at life and make up relationships--that happened and that's why this other thing happened--and we feel we have some control, or choice, because we UNDERSTAND. Why did that happen to me? It was my karma. Some combination of things happened somewhere in time and space and the result in my life is this. Is that true? Who knows? But I feel comforted having SOME KIND OF explanation. Without an idea like karma, life is just chaotic and random. It actually isn't, but that's how it looks to a self who sees itself as separate from everything else.

As a separate self, the illusion of separation, the illusion of INDIVIDUALITY, is held in place by karma, by a set of beliefs, habits, and assumptions that keep the world the same. It doesn't matter what goes on in life, my karma, my conditioned orientation to life, will see it the same way. Karma is like looking out of a pair of glasses that cause everything to look a particular way. The karmic glasses I have on make the world look frightening or friendly or overwhelming or hateful or whatever, and sure enough, everything that happens in life is seen in that particular way.

HERE IS THE SCENARIO:

You're going along, nothing particular is happening, nothing much is going on with you, and then something happens that you take personally. In an instant, you're upset.

Here is what I asked the class to do:

How did that happen? This is a big question. It is not an intellectual question. I'm asking you to scrutinize your reaction in your body, feelings, and mind. Where does it start? What is the "trigger"? Where is the first sensation of "taking it personally"? What is the first emotion? What is the first thought?

Responses

I have noticed this about the onset of being upset: I often have reactions to nothing. I am driving or looking at cookbooks or planting flowers, and I think about something, barely a complete

thought, and instantly there's a nasty feeling in my stomach, of not-good-enough-
going-to-fail-bad-
things-are-going-to-
happen terror. Lately,
my reaction has been
simply, "Oh, yeah,
that," and I go on with

the rest of the day. But I think it has quite a hold on me just the same.

Oh, IT has a big hold on everyone, most folks just don't see it--any of it. So, when I say egocentric, karmic conditioning has no life in the present and must draw you out of this moment into the past or future in order to experience itself as real, you know exactly what I mean. There you are doing something neutral, or even enjoyable, and BOOM, big dose of everything it takes to slam you out of the present and into the world of conditioning. What to do? Exactly what you're doing--notice it. Notice that everything that happens can be explained by the "out of the moment into conditioning" theory OR the "your world is crashing down, you'd better panic and go into misery as a response" theory. We can now consider which way we'd like to live our lives.

One "trigger" for taking something personally is a perceived put-down from a friend. I instantly feel attacked.

The first sensation is that my eyes feel full of tears; my face burns; my solar plexus starts to quiver.

The first emotion is embarrassment mixed with anger.

The first thought is astonishment: "Why did she say that? What did I do to deserve that treatment?"

Excellent work. Stay with it. As you watch, "space" will grow around these events. Memories will surface. You will see how you came to approach people this way. As you gain more distance and more clarity, other possibilities will open up. You will notice that you respond the same way to certain kinds of comments. You will see that sometimes you react and sometimes you don't. Eventually it will occur to you that your friend might be living in a completely different world, having a completely different life experience, and you might get curious about what that is.

I first feel upset about something, and then come thoughts such as, "That's bad. I didn't want that to happen. That's not fair." I feel sad or angry or anxious. Those negative feelings and thoughts can seem so overwhelming. Trying to replace negative with positive doesn't help, and I'm at the bottom of the pit before I know it. At that point, whatever originally triggered the feeling upset has become very personal. Is there a way not to be overwhelmed by feelings?

I remind people with, what I feel sure is, annoying regularity that if this practice were easy it would be more popular. Consider that, please. Look around and see what has thousands or even millions of "adherents." What do those things have in common? I would suggest that they all share the quality of people being exactly as they are while having something hopeful to believe. Very popular. Compare that with a practice that encourages people moment by moment to go up against, see through, and embrace the worst stuff in life. Not popular.

It is important to acknowledge that what you're doing is hard. It is not impossible. It is worthwhile. It will get easier. And, it is hard.

Feelings are overwhelming because we try to resist them. We attempt to hold them at bay and go about our lives. The pressure builds as we weaken and soon there's a collapse.

I have been watching how conditioning engages me in feeling upset. The process begins with a heavy, hot feeling in my chest and then moves behind my eyes (into my mind?), where I start feeling threatened because another person is expressing/ doing something that is contrary to my way of thinking/ believing. My first thought is "No, no, no!"

I was surprised to see the physical sensation--don't think I was ever aware of that heavy feeling before this class.

Stay with it. Those physical sensations, which are just sensations and have no meaning other than what we give them, are the beginning of great suffering and great freedom.

Today as I was walking to class, it started to rain. I was pleased with how I was dressed and furious at the rain for ruining my outfit. I thought about not taking it personally and tuned into the anger, frustration, sadness, etc. Then I thought, hey, why not make this a positive? Walking in the rain, pensive, enjoying the feel of it on my skin, the whole Gene Kelly thing.

Then I thought, no, that would be taking it personally, too. I don't think the idea is to buy into "positive thinking." So I just observed myself walking in the rain. Not trying to be happy. Noticing that I was frustrated and the tension in my shoulders.

This seems like I am playing mind games with myself. I am trying to just be, and I feel lost. I don't know what to be or how to be. I guess I don't know what's real anymore, if that makes sense. Did I miss the point of all of this?

I don't think you missed the point, I think what we're attempting is tricky given egocentric, karmic conditioning's stake in having us fail. Here is my encouragement until we meet again: Don't try to figure anything out, just notice everything. That thought is there and then that feeling and now a voice is saying something and then I'm thinking and now a voice is saying I don't get this... Meanwhile, keep breathing. As often as you can remember to do so, drop everything that is pulling your attention away and come back to your breath. Long, full, life-giving breath. Now a voice is saying I'm doing it wrong and I feel bad and now I'm thinking that maybe I was better off when I was totally asleep and now... Breathe!!!! Noticing everything, breathing regularly.

Overwhelm is present. I've just visited my family and been the recipient of my mother's verbal abuse once again. Over and over for the past 30 years, since my teens, I have tried to make sense of it. This class has helped me have some compassion for myself around it, but not yet for her. Some part of me is still "taking it personally" that I don't have the kind of mother ego believes I should have.

I used every tool I could remember and kept reading over these classes to try to regain a memory of my center, but the voices continue non-stop. I feel lost at sea with no life raft. I "know" so many things, have studied for so many years. Why am I still drowning in all this judgment and fear? It just seems that the waves keep coming and I'm gasping for breath.

It's an odd place we can find ourselves in, doing

work such as this. We know the right answers but still have trouble accepting them. I know that the right answer is to accept myself as I am. I know I need to learn to move into a place of compassionate, conscious awareness and embrace all that suffers, but there I am face to face with my parent, I go crazy, and then feel lost. Even though I know the right answer is acceptance of what is, as it is, I want to be different. I want to be over this. I want my life to work. I've done all the work to make my life work and, damn it, I want my life to work! The Zen term for this place is "rugged." It is hard, right in the middle of the fray, to be grateful that there are no short cuts.

IN OUR PRACTICE the definition of suffering is "wanting something to be other than the way it is." Pain exists. All sorts of things that we have the ability to see as bad and wrong exist in life. When we believe ourselves to be separate from life, when we hold an idea of how life should be and in comparing life as it is to our idea of how life should be, find life as it is lacking, we suffer. We suffer when we believe that life, as it is, is wrong. We suffer when we distance ourselves from life and judge that what is should not be.

Here is what I asked the class to do:

Please answer this question: If you didn't take anything personally, how would it be possible to suffer?

Responses

I don't know how anyone--including the guide and all liberated persons--could NOT want such things as war, rape, murder, child abuse, and infliction of pain on sentient beings to be different, as in nonexistent. How can you, if you can?

How can I not want life to be different from the way it is? Because I don't know what is going on with life. Because I don't know why life is the way it is. Because I don't KNOW that there is anything wrong with the way it is. Because I don't know that it would be better if it were in keeping with my egocentric perspective of "better." Because I don't know. That's one piece of it.

The other piece is that in my own experience, much of life that I did not want to be as it was, was the most helpful to me in terms of letting go of egocentric, center-of-the-universeness and opening up to conscious, compassionate awareness. At one point I so much did not want to live that I shot myself. There are laws against that! Whole, huge structures are set up to prevent that sort of behavior and to deal with those who do not comply. Those invested in those structures would have stopped me if they could have. They were not able to stop me, and I had the greatest turning point of my life. If they had been able to stop me, if my life had been allowed to go on as it was, in my heart of hearts I feel I would have been better off dead!

Do I WANT war, rape, murder, child abuse, and the inflicting of pain? Of course not. (And, I think it is good to keep in mind that my life has been, and is, devoted to work that MAY make a difference in those areas. That's what I do for twelve to fifteen hours a day, day in and day out, year after year. I offer you that perspective, not in defensiveness, but to ask you to consider if you can make that statement. I spend my life encouraging people to move away from an identification with egocentricity that would CAUSE them to engage in those practices, and regularly I get accused of being uncaring. Just something to consider.)

Do I want suffering in the world? Of course I do not. SUFFERING IN THE WORLD EXISTS. IT IS. I DID NOT CAUSE IT AND I CANNOT BRING ENOUGH JUDGMENT TO "OTHERS" TO MAKE IT GO AWAY. What I can do is end suffering in myself, live the most consciously compassionate and aware life I can manage, and be available to anyone who might say, How can I do that in my life?

Tonight, for probably the ten thousandth time, I took something personally, and began to have a nice little karmic fit. But this time, it suddenly occurred to me that this had *absolutely nothing* to do with what was going on at all. Several statements popped into my mind that I *felt* more than *heard*. I'm sure you'll recognize them: "The only thing that wants/needs defending is egocentric, karmic conditioning." "Conditioning *wants* to suffer." "Content is irrelevant."

It was like being awakened from a nightmare. And in a matter of moments, I went from rage to laughter. It felt like letting the air out of a balloon. I no longer cared at all what was said, what did or did not happen   I was breathing, and determined not to support or defend ego in any way. And I can't tell you how exhilarating this feels! It's like an enormous burden has been lifted from my shoulders.

Yes! That is one of those things I wish I could bottle and give away on every street corner around the world. Cling to conditioned beliefs, emotions, and behaviors and suffer. Let go and be fully, joyously, gloriously alive. You have all that life force coursing through you. You can enjoy it or you can give it to egocentricity and suffer over how ego uses that energy to make you miserable. Fit or bliss? The choice is always there. Same energy, you can let conditioning trap it in suffering or take a long deep breath, let it go, and grin from ear to ear.

All I see right now is that as much as I am open to life, life is experienced in me. When I close to part of life, based on fear, I suffer. If I am not aware of when I close, I become separated and lost. The more aware I become of what closes me off from my life, the more choice I have to be one with life and there is less suffering.

Well said. That is the sequence: egocentricity is

fear, ego feels afraid, ego closes down, you feel alone and lost. As you recognize that sequence, you find that the recognition IS the reversal. You notice that you're feeling lost and alone except that in the noticing, you're there and no longer feel alone. Because you're present, you're not lost, you're here! When you're here, with yourself, the very process of being present IS opening. You're here, present, aware, open and there is nothing to fear. It feels like magic (which it is!) and it is pure logic.

SMALL CHILDREN and animals are endearing and charming (as well as courageous and heroic) largely because they take nothing in life personally. They will try anything, dance and jump around unselfconsciously, not assume doing a thing well is a criterion for doing it, and generally put enjoying themselves ahead of standards. Before a certain age children don't even know that people believe there are certain standards which must be met. They don't know there is a "right" way for things to be and therefore don't know when something is "wrong." Before a certain age, even if it becomes obvious that something is not working, the child does not assume it has anything to do with itself.

Here is what I asked the class to do:

What is possible for you in your life when you don't take things personally that are not possible when you do? In other words, how does taking

things personally limit you, and how would not
taking things personally free you?

Responses

It happened. I caught ego trying to manipulate a friend's anger
at me into "taking it personally" and was able to watch and not
respond inappropriately. I'm letting it go. I sent her an e-mail
saying, "All's well that end's well."

Good for you. The "teflon school of karma
removal." Someone comes at you with a load of
what would be big karmic yuck, and you just let
it hit the front of your teflon-protected person,
and it slides to the ground never to be picked up
by anyone. What a kindness to us all. Thank
you.

Last night during meditation, a kaleidoscope of failures and
missed opportunities spun through my awareness. And what
came to me was how vicious this show was, and, as you
have said, the force behind it all—be it karmic conditioning, the
"devil," or whatever we would like to call it—is interested *only* in
causing suffering. The content may have been tailor-made for

me, but in watching it change from subject to subject, as if trying to find something that could suck me in totally, it struck me that *none of it has anything to do with me at all.* I could be anyone at all. The content could be anything at all. There's nothing to take personally, regardless of what I've done or not done, said or not, even who I am.

That's it. How freeing to realize that! There's a story told about the Buddha: A young mother came to him, hysterical with grief, carrying the body of her dead child. The Buddha attempted to explain to her about life and death, impermanence, egolessness, and suffering, but she could not hear a word. How could this happen? How could her child die? Why did this happen to her? Finally the Buddha asked her to go out into the community and find a family to whom nothing like this had happened. All day she went from home to home, asking about their tragedies, and hearing their stories. At the end of the day she returned to the Buddha, ready to release her child and begin the process of letting go.

None of this is personal. Not the circumstances of life, not the karmic conditioning that would have us believe that life should be different from the way it is. What is is. We cannot change what is, but this is what I've noticed: No matter what life may hand us, conscious, compassionate awareness makes everything easier.

Today as I was meditating I felt uncomfortable, out of balance, then I compensated for that by tensing my body. I became so tense that it was painful, and I wanted to stop meditating. Instead, I stopped taking the tension personally—then it became just another feeling, not something that I was supposed to take care of. I dropped the sense of responsibility that I usually carry for my physical comfort and became responsible only for noticing the feeling. It stopped being "my" feeling and became just "a" feeling. Then it was easy to continue meditating and actually to be even more aware of the feeling of discomfort, which was somehow no longer uncomfortable.

Yes. Then it just is what is, like the weather. If there is no "I" there to take it personally, to hold beliefs about how it should be that it's not, if there is just noticing it, there is nothing

211

wrong, and hence, no problem. No suffering and no one to suffer. Very relaxing.

A Final Encouragement

JOY

THE NATURAL RESULT of seeing through our beliefs and assumptions, the conditioned ways we approach life and take it personally, is an openness, a spaciousness that was previously filled with illusions and misinformation. Another word for this open and spaciousness is <u>emptiness</u>, which can sound like lack or loss. And it's true that it is a loss for egocentricity, a loss of its control over our lives. But it's not a loss of anything, it's an emptiness that is actually a fullness, abundance, plentitude, all that is, a world of limitless possibility. Another name for that spaciousness is <u>joy</u>. That's why we say joy is what's there when you stop doing everything else. "Everything else" encompasses assuming, acting out of habit, trying to control, judging, knowing, believing, and all other aspects of our conditioned reaction to life, including trying to be joyful.

Here is what I asked the class to do:

Please sit back, relax, close your eyes, and spend a few moments focusing on the breath before you begin this guided imagery. When you're ready, recall a time when you felt joy. Give yourself all the time you need to allow an image, a memory, to come to you of a time when you were feeling joy.

Sometimes people experience joy in happy or pleasant circumstances, sometimes when they feel gratitude. Perhaps joy comes with the experience of loving or being loved unconditionally. Or you might associate joy with feeling accepted or appreciated. Whatever the circumstances, let yourself return to that moment of joy.

Notice how joy feels in your body. Where in your body do you feel joy? Can you let the feeling fill your whole body?

Consider now, what is the color of joy? What is the texture, the shape, the size, the feel, the taste, the aroma of joy?

Imagine now that the color of joy is all around you. For as far as you can imagine, all the air is the color of joy. Can you see that color all around you? Everything is surrounded by and resting in the color of joy. With each breath you are breathing in the color of joy... breathing joy in, breathing joy out... your body filled with joy, surrounded by joy, supported by joy... enveloped in joy... no inside, no outside... nothing separate, nothing left out, nothing other... all joy.

Stay with that experience for as long as you like, and then when you feel ready, slowly, gently bring your attention back to the room where you are. Allow your breath to deepen, wiggle your fingers and your toes, wiggle your lips and smile, and when you feel ready, open your eyes.

Responses

The joyful moment I recalled was when my 11-year-old son showed me a letter he wrote as a homework assignment, where he described his most important person—and it was me! He wrote many sweet things about me, and I didn't know he felt that way, since we sometimes fight over this or that.

I am a bit confused here though. You said that joy happens when we let go of having to believe something. My mind is telling me that the reason I felt joy was because I realized (belief change) that my son loves me a lot. Is my mind playing tricks on me?

Number one, I hate to be a boring old stickler for details, but I'm going to ask you to go back and find the place where I said, "joy happens when we let go of having to believe something." Now, maybe I did say that (I don't always listen carefully to myself), but I'm wondering if what I said was more like, "Joy is what's there when we stop doing everything else." Number two, it's not hard to be happy when we get something we really want. Number three, I hope you will look closely at the process you identify as, "I realized (belief change) that my son loves me a lot." Was the experience you had actually about "belief"? What will happen the next time you fight over this or that? Will you then believe he doesn't love you? I wonder if the words belief, think, and conclude are being used interchangeably, and if they mean the same thing to you. Remember that we're not looking for answers, we're learning to pay attention and be open to a larger picture than the one we're conditioned to see.

I stayed with the joy exercise for a long time, remembering different times of joy in my life. To my surprise, every time I got a vivid memory of a joyful experience in my head and in my body, I began to cry. If I were to try to put words to the tears, loss was part of it, like I felt that I had experienced exquisite joy before and now it is lost. But in some other way, it was simply overwhelming that I could re-experience that joy. Anyway, I just flooded up with tears again and again and I could not go further with the exercise. What's up with that?

Well, of course, I don't know what's up with that, but that never stops me from projecting!

In my experience, when that happens to me, I am letting go. The relief of letting go of tensing up against life produces tears.

Here is my question: What is it about being flooded up with tears that would keep you from proceeding with joy?

Whenever I want to conjure up joy, I imagine I am powder skiing. My body is buried in light powder up to my thighs, and I am moving my body up and down in rhythm, surfing through a white cloud. I am acutely aware of the contrast of snow against the dark green trees, the cold against my face, and the very rhythm of life. I let go of where my skis are (because I can't see them, anyway) and I just undulate in response to the hidden terrain. There is no "I", there is only now, only this moment, only here, only this, only breath, only heart beat, only life, only everything. All semblance of control is abandoned--to try and control anything in powder is to lose control. I feel such ecstasy, my heart is bursting. At the end of the day, my face is tired from constant grinning ear-to-ear. I often think to myself at the end of a day skiing, that I could die right then and there and it would be perfectly fine. And the idea of death is no longer frightening. How could it be-- after a day of being completely alive?

There is an old expression in Zen, the author of which I cannot recall, that goes, "When we realize our inherent enlightenment in the morning, we do not mind dying in the afternoon." I have no doubt that you understand the truth of this.

The awareness of joy feels like it's in my whole body; it's like my whole body is breathing and there is no barrier to anything around me. Somehow "I" is connected to ALL in those moments of joy.

Yes. Here is what I would ask you to consider. It is not that "somehow 'I' is connected to all in those moments of joy." In those moments you are actually having an experience of the absence of an "I," an experience of nothing that is separate from joy.

IT IS MY EXPERIENCE that there is nothing wrong with anyone. How can that be? Because there is only life and by definition there is no room in "only" for something "other." There is only life. You are life. There is no alternative. You are not a mistake. There is nothing wrong with you. You are caught in the death grip of a delusion. As soon as you see that, you are free. What you believe is not true. As soon as you see that, you are free. What the voices are saying to you is not true. As soon as you see that, you are free. And here is the most essential piece of information I can offer you: You will never see it as long as you look to conditioned mind--for anything! If you can spend even a very short period of time in the present, you will see what actually IS. And you will never be willing to go back to believing what the voices tell you.

But you have to have the experience for yourself. I can point at it; I cannot make you have it. Alas, I cannot even give it to you.

I wish I could. My great comfort is the assurance that each of us, when we have suffered enough, has all we need to end suffering.

My deepest wish
is that you will not stop until
you have proved this
for yourself.

LIVING COMPASSION

To find out about our work with orphans in Zambia
and about purchasing gift cards and other products
that support that work,
visit www.livingcompassion.org.

* * *

ZEN MONASTERY PEACE CENTER

For a schedule of workshops and retreats and a list of our
meditation groups across the country,
contact us in one of the following ways.

Website: www.livingcompassion.org
Email: thezencenter@livingcompassion.org
Telephone: 209-728-0860
Fax: 209-728-0861

Zen Monastery Peace Center
P.O. Box 1756
Murphys, CA 95247

* * *

CHERI HUBER

For a schedule of retreats
and online classes with Cheri Huber
and archives of her call-in radio show,
visit www.cherihuber.com.

There Is Nothing Wrong With You
An Extraordinary Eight Day Retreat
based on the book
There Is Nothing Wrong With You: Going Beyond Self-Hate
by Cheri Huber

Inside each of us is a "persistent voice of discontent." It is constantly critical of life, the world, and almost everything we say and do. As children, in order to survive, we learned to listen to this voice and believe what it says.

This retreat, held at the beautiful Zen Monastery Peace Center near Murphys, California, in the western foothills of the Sierra Nevada, is eight days of looking directly at how we have been rejecting and punishing ourselves and discovering how to let that go. Through a variety of exercises and periods of group processing, participants will gain a clearer perspective on how they live their lives and on how to find compassion for themselves and others.

This work is challenging, joyous, fulfilling, scary, courageous, demanding, freeing, loving, kind, and compassionate—compassionate toward yourself and everyone you will ever know.

For information on attending, contact:
Living Compassion/Zen Monastery Peace Center
P.O. Box 1756
Murphys, CA 95247
Ph.: 209-728-0860
Fax: 209-728-0861
Email: thezencenter@livingcompassion.org
Website: www.livingcompassion.org

BOOKS FROM CHERI HUBER

Published by Keep It Simple Books

All titles are available through your local bookstore.

(Distributed by Independent Publishers Group, Chicago)